Whispers of Innocence

Whispers of Innocence

Toddler's Tooth Tales

Sam Loray

Spectra Enterprise

Contents

Table Of Content   **1**

Introduction   **3**

Chapter 1   **6**

Chapter 2   **23**

Chapter 3   **40**

Chapter 4   **61**

Chapter 5   **79**

Chapter 6   **97**

Chapter 7   **118**

Table Of Content

Introduction

Chapter 1: The First Whisper
1.1. Birth of the First Tooth
1.2. The excitement and anticipation
1.3. Parental reactions and celebrations

Chapter 2: Tiny Teeth, Big Dreams
2.1. The Toddler's World
2.2. Exploring the early years of childhood
2.3. Symbolism of milk teeth in innocence

Chapter 3: Lost and Found
3.1. Adventures of the Tooth Fairy
3.2. Tradition and folklore surrounding lost teeth
3.3. The mysterious exchange: tooth for a treasure

Chapter 4: The Language of Smiles
4.1. Communicating through Grins
4.2. Toddler's toothy smiles as a form of expression
4.3. Parental decoding of baby talk

Chapter 5: Gentle Beginnings
5.1. Nurturing the Milk Teeth
5.2. Dental care for toddlers
5.3. Milestones in tooth development

Chapter 6: Ivory Keepsakes
6.1. Preserving Childhood Memories

6.2. Creating keepsakes with fallen teeth

6.3. The sentimental value of baby teeth

Chapter 7: Tooth Tales Around the World

7.1. Cultural Perspectives

7.2. Variations in tooth-related traditions globally

7.3. Uniqueness and commonalities in diverse cultures

Introduction

In the tranquil domains of youth, where guiltlessness rules and each disclosure is a wonder, there exists a mystical orchestra of murmurs that reverberate through the hallways of time. This orchestra is made out of the stories twirled around the fragile, vaporous fortunes that decorate the mouths of little children - their milk teeth. In "Murmurs of Blamelessness: Baby's Tooth Stories," we set out on an enthralling excursion through the charming universe of life as a youngster, where the development, misfortune, and imagery of these minuscule, ivory ponders weave an embroidery of recollections and dreams.

As we adventure into the core of this story, it becomes obvious that the enchanted falsehoods not simply in the actual rise of a kid's most memorable tooth however in the immaterial embodiment that encompasses it. Every tooth, a messenger of another stage in the baby's turn of events, conveys with it a murmur of blamelessness - a quiet decree of the remarkable excursion that is youth. It is in the expectation of that first tooth, the festival of ensuing appearances, and the mixed goodbyes to these transient sidekicks that the pith of this story unfurls.

The primary section unfurls like the fragile petals of a blooming blossom, catching the invigorating minutes when the main tooth gets through the gums. Guardians, gatekeepers, and relatives become observers to this striking achievement, stamping a natural change as well as the beginning of a long lasting excursion loaded up with giggling, bliss, and disclosure. A festival rises above social and geological limits, resounding with the general topic of parental unrivaled delight in seeing their youngster's development.

However, past the rawness of these arising teeth lies a more profound investigation of the baby's reality in the subsequent part. Inside the domains of blamelessness, interest, and limitless creative mind, these little teeth become devices for eating as well as instruments of correspondence. Toddlerhood is when grins become a language, and the energetic smiles of the little ones say a lot, rising above the requirement for words. It is in these early articulations that the story tracks down its mood, fitting with the general language of life as a youngster euphoria.

As we dig further into the story, the third part unwinds the captivating legends encompassing the lost teeth, where the Tooth Pixie arises as a supernatural person in the baby's universe. Across societies, the custom of setting a fallen tooth under the pad, anticipating the nighttime visit of the Tooth Pixie bearing a minuscule fortune, adds a bit of wizardry to the standard. This well established custom turns into a scaffold between the substantial and the fantastical, encouraging a feeling of marvel that penetrates the little child's insight.

The murmurs of honesty keep on reverberating in the fourth section as we investigate the special language of grins, unraveling the subtleties of correspondence through energetic smiles. Guardians become adroit mediators of their baby's implicit words, making a solid bond that rises above verbal articulations. It is inside these common grins that the excellence of life as a parent and the corresponding delight of a kid's giggling track down a significant association.

Delicate starting points and the supporting of milk teeth become the overwhelming focus in the fifth section, accentuating the significance of dental consideration in the early years. In the midst of the delicate brushing and periodic getting teeth challenges, guardians become watchmen of these fragile fortunes, encouraging a feeling of obligation and care. This section fills in as an aide for guardians, offering bits of knowledge into keeping up with the wellbeing and prosperity of these valuable images of guiltlessness.

As the story unfurls, the 6th part presents the idea of saving cherished, lifelong recollections through the tokens made with fallen teeth. Whether it be a little, painstakingly named envelope or a capriciously designed tooth pixie box, these mementos become unmistakable relics of a temporary stage in the youngster's life. Every tooth, a small time case, embodies the pith of a particular second in the kid's development, turning into an esteemed keepsake for both youngster and parent the same.

The worldwide viewpoint becomes the dominant focal point in the seventh part, digging into the different social practices and customs related with milk teeth. From the energetic jokes of the Tooth Mouse in Spain to the representative contributions of teeth to the divine beings in different Asian societies, the account investigates the wealth and assortment of tooth-related legends. This social woven artwork adds profundity to the tales as well as highlights the all inclusiveness of the encounters shared by guardians and youngsters all over the planet.

As the account advances, the eighth section tends to the difficulties and achievements experienced during the getting teeth process. Guardians are offered commonsense counsel and bits of knowledge into exploring the occasionally turbulent excursion of getting teeth, transforming difficulties into open doors for development and holding. This section fills in as a consoling aide, recognizing the common encounters of guardians while giving a strong voice to those exploring this stage interestingly.

The 10th part denotes a powerful change, zeroing in on the transformation from milk teeth to long-lasting smiles. As the last milk tooth says goodbye, the story catches the self-contradicting snapshots of this progress to adulthood. It represents the actual development of the youngster as well as the advancement of their character, character, and the remarkable engraving of their experience growing up.

In the finishing up parts, the story reflects upon the all-encompassing subjects of experience growing up and the murmurs of honesty that reverberate all through. The vaporous idea of these tooth stories fills in as a powerful sign of the brief idea of life as a youngster, provoking perusers to relish the valuable minutes and commend the excellence found in the easiest delights. The epilog integrates the strings of the account, underscoring the never-ending sorcery that lives in the murmurs of blamelessness, epitomized in the delicate stories of baby's tooth processes.

"Murmurs of Honesty: Baby's Tooth Stories" isn't only an assortment of stories; it is a festival of the widespread experience of young life. A tribute to the giggling reverberations through energetic smiles, the common snapshots of satisfaction and disclosure, and the ageless wizardry that dwells in the murmurs of blamelessness. Through these stories, perusers are welcome to leave on a nostalgic excursion, rediscovering the charm that encompasses the littlest, yet significantly critical, achievements of youth.

Chapter 1

The First Whisper

In the tranquil support of outset, where the world is a delicate bedtime song and each coo is a commitment of disclosure, the excursion of a youngster's most memorable tooth unfurls like a sensitive bud blooming into full blossom. "The Main Murmur" is a part that epitomizes the significant meaning of this underlying dental achievement, where the rise of the primary tooth turns into an ensemble of delight, wonder, and parental pride.

The account starts with the unpretentious signs that messenger the looming appearance of the primary tooth. It is a period set apart by the delicate distress of getting teeth, where small gums, when smooth, presently bear the delicate stirrings of a tooth's enlivening. Guardians become receptive to the unpretentious changes in their baby's way of behaving - the expanded slobber, a periodic particularity, and the voracious longing to bite on anything reachable. These are the prefaces to the main murmur, the expectation that forms in the hearts of guardians as they anticipate the rise of that first, silvery bud.

As the principal tooth gets through the gums, a pivotal event unfurls, rising above the organic into the domain of the profoundly close to home. The part catches the obvious fervor that pervades the family when the primary tooth shows up, changing the ordinary into the unprecedented. There is an unquestionable bliss in the revelation, a practically respectful amazement as guardians wonder about this minuscule, yet fantastic, demonstration of their kid's development.

The meaning of the principal tooth stretches out past its actual sign; it turns into an image of strength and perseverance. The baby, when completely reliant upon fluid sustenance, presently has the necessary resources to investigate new surfaces and flavors. The principal tooth is a messenger of the progress from unadulterated milk to a more extensive culinary world, denoting a urgent second in the kid's turn of events. This culinary investigation turns into a common encounter for both parent and kid, an excursion of shared disclosure that ties them in the basic demonstration of supporting.

In the midst of the festival, there is an affirmation of the transitory idea of these early achievements. The principal tooth is an update that youth is an embroidery woven with fleeting strings, every second to be valued before it gives approach to the following. Amidst parental celebration, there is a propensity of wistfulness for the child who once fit cozily in their arms, presently embellished with the image of thriving freedom.

"The Principal Murmur" isn't simply a festival of the actual development of a tooth; an investigation of the close to home scene goes with this achievement. A story dives into the profound well of parental feelings - the pride in seeing their kid's development, the wonderment at the versatility of small creatures, and the acknowledgment that every tooth is a venturing stone towards an eventual fate of vast conceivable outcomes.

Past the familial circle, the principal tooth holds social and cultural importance. In many societies, the presence of the principal tooth is set apart by ceremonies and customs that mirror the local area's aggregate affirmation of the kid's entrance into another period of life. It is a common festival, supporting the interconnected-ness of ages and the repeating idea of life.

The part likewise investigates the job of fables and odd notions encompassing the primary tooth. From the conviction that the primary tooth ought to be covered to areas of strength for advance, teeth in the future to the possibility that how the tooth arises impacts the kid's character, these social subtleties add layers of significance to the basic demonstration of getting teeth. It is a union of the natural and the social, where science and custom dance together as one.

However, in the midst of the delight and social festivals, there is an affirmation of the difficulties that go with getting teeth. The distress and incidental tears become piece of the account, highlighting the weakness of early stages. It is a dem-onstration of the strength of both youngster and parent, exploring the turbulent rushes of getting teeth with persistence and love.

As the part unfurls, it additionally investigates the job of the more distant family and the local area in commending the principal tooth. Grandparents, aunt-ies, uncles, and companions generally become necessary characters in this common story. The main tooth turns into a collective accomplishment, a wellspring of happiness that waves through the interconnected snare of connections.

The imagery of the main tooth stretches out past the close family and local area; it reverberations in the more extensive social and verifiable setting. From the beginning of time, the principal tooth has been portrayed in workmanship, writing, and legends as an image of honesty, weakness, and the recurrent idea of life. From old legends to cutting edge writing, the main tooth possesses a venerated place in the aggregate creative mind, rising above individual encounters to turn into a general theme.

"The Main Murmur" isn't just a relating of actual occasions; an investigation of the multi-layered layers encompass the development of a youngster's most memorable tooth. A story winds around together the organic, close to home, social, and cultural elements of this achievement, welcoming perusers to ponder the significant idea of youth.

In the end passages of this part, there is a feeling of reflection on the extraordinary force of the principal tooth. An image resounds a long ways past the bounds of the nursery, reverberating in the hearts of guardians, parental figures, and networks. The main tooth is a murmur that resonates through time, interfacing ages and winding around the embroidery of shared human encounters.

As the story of "The Principal Murmur" attracts to a nearby, it has a permanent impression of the fragile magnificence saw as in the least complex of minutes. It is a tribute to the murmurs of euphoria, marvel, and cherish that go with the rise of a youngster's most memorable tooth - a murmur that rises above the limits of language, culture, and time. In the orchestra of youth, the principal tooth is the initial note, making way for a long period of songs yet to unfurl.

The reverberation of "The Principal Murmur" stretches out past the quick limits of the family and local area, venturing into the domains of logical request and mental investigation. The rise of the main tooth isn't just an actual peculiarity however a mental and formative achievement that enamors specialists and youngster clinicians the same.

Inside the logical talk, the ejection of the primary tooth is examined as a significant part of a kid's formative direction. Dental specialists and pediatricians fastidiously screen this occasion as a mark of the kid's general wellbeing and prosperity. It turns into a substantial proportion of the kid's capacity to flourish, checking the coming of biting and discourse as well as representing the preparation of the body to advance from earliest stages to the little child years.

Mentally, the primary tooth fills in as a foundation in the underpinning of a kid's mindfulness. The attention to the actual changes in their body, combined with the responses and festivities of their parental figures, adds to the development of early self-idea. The uplifting feedback and delight related with the main tooth make a feeling of achievement and approval for the kid, laying the preparation for a solid confidence.

The section likewise digs into the mind boggling dance among nature and support during this stage. It investigates how parental figures, through their reactions and cooperations, assume a urgent part in forming the youngster's view of this achievement. The reverberation of the primary tooth in the relational intricacies isn't just an organic event yet a socio-close to home occasion that impacts the social elements inside the nuclear family.

Moreover, "The Main Murmur" examines the more extensive cultural ramifications of this apparently standard yet significantly critical occasion. The festival of the principal tooth turns into a social marker, building up cultural qualities and customs. A common story rises above individual encounters, interfacing families through ages and cultivating a feeling of progression and heritage.

In writing and mainstream society, the primary tooth frequently winds up woven into accounts that investigate topics of development, development, and the progression of time. From old legends representing soul changing experiences to current youngsters' accounts, the primary tooth takes on an emblematic job that resounds with crowds, everything being equal. It turns into a general theme, a demonstration of the repetitive idea of life and the unending pattern of birth, development, and reestablishment.

"The Main Murmur" doesn't avoid recognizing the subtleties and difficulties that go with this upbeat event. Getting teeth, with its distress and periodic restless evenings, is depicted as a common encounter that joins guardians all over the planet. The section carefully recognizes the versatility of both parent and youngster during this stage, underscoring the strength got from the solidarity of the familial bond.

As the story unfurls, it winds around a rich embroidery of different social practices and convictions encompassing the primary tooth. Whether it be the Hindu practice of putting a silver coin in the mouth of a newborn child with the principal tooth or the Japanese custom of observing Haguichi, the primary tooth celebration, these social subtleties add profundity and variety to the story. It is a festival of the kaleidoscope of human encounters, where the principal tooth turns into a material painted with the shifted tints of social legacy.

Inside the familial setting, grandparents expect an exceptional job in the festival of the main tooth. Their insight, frequently saturated with custom, turns into a directing power, conferring experiences and customs that add layers of importance to the familial story. Grandparents become the torchbearers of social heritage, passing down stories, customs, and the meaning of the primary tooth starting with one age then onto the next.

The end sections of "The Main Murmur" embrace a tone of reflection, welcoming perusers to consider the significant excursion implanted in this apparently little occasion. It coaxes them to look past the surface and perceive the mind boggling exchange of science, feeling, culture, and history that combines in the rise of a youngster's most memorable tooth.

As perusers navigate the story scene of "The Primary Murmur," they are not just observers yet dynamic members in a general story of development, love, and shared humankind. The main tooth turns into an illustration for the murmurs of guiltlessness that reverberation through the passages of youth, leaving a permanent engraving on the hearts of the individuals who demonstrate the veracity of its rise.

Generally, "The Primary Murmur" is a tribute to the verse tracked down in the standard, an investigation of the remarkable inside the apparently commonplace snapshots of life. It welcomes perusers to adjust their faculties to the nuances of satisfaction, marvel, and association that radiate from the primary tooth - a murmur that resounds across societies, ages, and the vast spread of human experience.

1.1. Birth of the First Tooth

In the consecrated domain of earliest stages, where each coo is an ensemble and each look holds the commitment of disclosure, the section named "Birth of the Principal Tooth" unfurls with the expectation of a delicate suggestion. This part is an excursion through the fragile limit of a kid's dental turn of events, catching the quintessence existing apart from everything else when the principal tooth, similar to a modest bud, shows up.

At the beginning, the story digs into the unobtrusive messengers of getting teeth, those underlying signs that envoy the looming development of a tooth. Guardians, receptive to the subtleties of their newborn child's way of behaving, notice the indications - the expanded slobber, the biting on fingers or toys, and an intermittent fastidiousness.

These are the introductions to the stupendous appearance, the unobtrusive murmurs that signal the change occurring inside the little, developing mouth.

As the main tooth gets through the gums, the air becomes accused of unmistakable fervor. This second, frequently anticipated eagerly, marks a physiological achievement as well as a strong move toward the excursion of being a parent. The section catches the sheer euphoria that saturates the family as parental figures give testimony regarding this small scale supernatural occurrence - a tooth, when secret underneath the gums, presently presented to the world.

The meaning of the main tooth stretches out past its actual rise; it turns into an image of development, strength, and the unfurling story of a youngster's turn of events. It is a demonstration of the marvelous idea of life, where an apparently unremarkable occasion turns into a wellspring of miracle and festivity. Guardians, at this time, become stewards of an excursion, exploring the unfamiliar waters of early stages with a mix of wonderment and obligation.

The main tooth, frequently a lower focal incisor, becomes the overwhelming focus in the oral cavity as well as in the familial story. This particular tooth turns into a point of convergence for familial pride and shared satisfaction. In its appearance, there is an acknowledgment of the unyielding section of time, as the newborn child changes from the sticky grins of early earliest stages to the thriving dental scene of toddlerhood.

Past the close family, the part investigates the mutual part of praising the introduction of the principal tooth. Grandparents, aunties, uncles, and dear companions become necessary characters in this common account, each contributing their extraordinary point of view to the aggregate happiness. The principal tooth turns into a collective victory, supporting the interconnectedness of connections and the public idea of familial festivals.

The account then, at that point, unfurls to investigate the convergence of social customs and the introduction of the primary tooth. Various societies and social orders have differing customs and convictions encompassing this achievement, adding profundity and variety to the all-encompassing account. Whether it be a stylized gala, a formal contribution, or a conventional tune, the introduction of the main tooth turns into an embroidery woven with the strings of social legacy.

In the more extensive cultural setting, the primary tooth ends up implanted in logical request and pediatric talk. Dental specialists and medical services experts screen the ejection of the primary tooth as a sign of the kid's general wellbeing and formative direction. The part momentarily addresses the logical meaning of this occasion, remembering it as in excess of a beguiling visual marker yet as an essential part of a youngster's physiological movement.

Mentally, the introduction of the main tooth turns into a significant investigation of mindfulness. The consciousness of another presence inside the mouth, combined with the responses and festivities of guardians, adds to the early development of a youngster's self-idea. It isn't simply an actual occasion; it is a mental arousing, an acknowledgment of one's changing body and the world's reactions to it.

Amidst festivity and social observances, the part doesn't avoid recognizing the difficulties that frequently go with getting teeth. The distress, infrequent restless evenings, and the requirement for extra relieving become vital pieces of this common experience. It is a depiction of weakness and flexibility, where both parent and kid explore the blustery oceans of getting teeth with persistence and love.

The part then, at that point, winds around the encounters of more distant family individuals, particularly grandparents, into the story. Grandparents, with their abundance of involvement and intelligence, become significant supporters of the festival. They might deliver revered customs, share tales from their own nurturing ventures, and give a feeling of congruity and inheritance to the familial story encompassing the introduction of the principal tooth.

As the story unfurls, it embraces the subtleties and difficulties that go with the euphoric event. The primary tooth isn't simply an image of development yet an impression of the recurrent idea of life. It is a delicate update that each stage in a youngster's improvement is transient, encouraging parental figures to esteem the current second before it changes into a memory.

Inside the familial setting, the introduction of the main tooth cultivates a more profound association among guardians and their kid. A common encounter reinforces the bond, making a repository of shared recollections and minutes. The kid's most memorable tooth turns into a foundation in the development of a familial account, a story retold with affection and sentimentality as the youngster develops.

The account then, at that point, turns to the investigation of social practices and convictions that encompass the introduction of the main tooth. From the Chinese custom of red egg and ginger gatherings to the Mexican practice of a "preliminary diente" festivity, the part enlightens the rich variety of worldwide practices. It is a festival of the variety of human encounters, every practice adding a layer of importance to the all inclusive story of tooth rise.

Besides, the part recognizes the representative weight that the principal tooth conveys in writing and mainstream society. It turns into an illustration for development, development, and the progression of time. From old legends to cutting edge youngsters' accounts, the main tooth takes on a representative job that resounds with crowds, everything being equal. It turns into an all inclusive theme, a demonstration of the repeating idea of life and the ceaseless pattern of birth, development, and restoration.

The end sections of "Birth of the Principal Tooth" embrace a tone of reflection, welcoming perusers to mull over the significant excursion implanted in this apparently little occasion. It urges them to perceive the many-sided transaction of science, feeling, culture, and history that joins in the development of a youngster's most memorable tooth.

As perusers cross the story scene of "Birth of the Principal Tooth," they are not simple onlookers but rather dynamic members in a general story of development, love, and shared mankind. The primary tooth turns into an illustration for the murmurs of life, the mind boggling dance of starting points and endings that shape the human experience. It is a tribute to the verse tracked down in the normal, an investigation of the phenomenal inside the apparently unremarkable snapshots of life.

The account of "Birth of the Principal Tooth" further unfurls into the complex dance among nature and sustain during this critical period of outset. The part investigates how parental figures, through their reactions and communications, assume a pivotal part in forming the kid's view of this achievement. The reverberation of the principal tooth in relational peculiarities isn't exclusively a natural event yet a socio-close to home occasion that significantly impacts the social texture inside the nuclear family.

Besides, the part unpredictably winds around together the encounters of the two guardians, making an embroidery of shared liabilities and delights. A story perceives the unmistakable jobs played by moms and fathers in the festival of the primary tooth, recognizing the cooperative endeavors that add to the supporting of a youngster's development. In this orchestra of life as a parent, the primary tooth turns into a tune created by the amicable association of providing care jobs.

As the account unfurls, it stretches out its look to the more extensive cultural ramifications of this apparently standard yet significantly critical occasion. The festival of the principal tooth turns into a social marker, building up cultural qualities and customs. A common story rises above individual encounters, inter-facing families through ages and cultivating a feeling of coherence and heritage. The introduction of the principal tooth, in this specific situation, turns into a microcosm of the aggregate human experience, a sign of the common excursion through the patterns of life.

In writing and mainstream society, the principal tooth frequently winds up woven into stories that investigate subjects of development, development, and the progression of time. From old legends representing soul changing experiences to current kids' accounts, the principal tooth takes on a representative job that reverberates with crowds, everything being equal.

It turns into a widespread theme, a demonstration of the repeating idea of life and the ceaseless pattern of birth, development, and restoration. In doing as such, the story perceives the social and verifiable aspects that raise the introduction of the primary tooth past an individual achievement to an image implanted in the shared mindset.

Inside the familial setting, grandparents expect a unique job in the festival of the main tooth. Their insight, frequently saturated with custom, turns into a directing power, granting experiences and customs that add layers of importance to the familial story. Grandparents become the torchbearers of social inheritance, passing down stories, ceremonies, and the meaning of the main tooth starting with one age then onto the next. In this intergenerational trade, the primary tooth turns into a scaffold that associates the past, present, and future.

The account then, at that point, nimbly explores the encounters of more distant family individuals, particularly aunties and uncles, advancing the embroidered artwork of festivity. Their jobs, set apart by energy and backing, add to the public bliss encompassing the main tooth. It is an update that the introduction of a kid's most memorable tooth isn't restricted to the family unit however stretches out its waves to embrace the more extensive connection organization.

As the part unfurls, it embraces the subtleties and difficulties that go with the cheerful event. The principal tooth isn't simply an image of development however an impression of the repeating idea of life. It is a delicate update that each stage in a kid's improvement is transient, encouraging parental figures to esteem the current second before it changes into a memory. This affirmation of temporariness adds a layer of impact to the festival, welcoming an intelligent interruption in the midst of the cheerful celebration.

In featuring the mutual part of commending the primary tooth, the story catches the aggregate pride and shared satisfaction that saturate the familial and social circles. The main tooth turns into a public victory, building up the inter-connectedness of connections and the common idea of familial festivals. In this common celebration, the section perceives the widespread reverberation of the primary tooth as an image of fresh starts and the progression of life.

The account then, at that point, nimbly changes to investigate the convergence of social customs and the introduction of the primary tooth. Various societies and social orders have differing customs and convictions encompassing this achievement, adding profundity and variety to the general story. Whether it be a stylized dining experience, a ceremonial contribution, or a customary tune, the introduction of the principal tooth turns into an embroidery woven with the strings of social legacy. It is a festival of the variety of human encounters, every custom adding a layer of significance to the all inclusive story of tooth development.

Moreover, the part recognizes the emblematic weight that the main tooth conveys in writing and mainstream society. It turns into a similitude for development, development, and the progression of time. From old legends to cutting edge youngsters' accounts, the primary tooth takes on an emblematic job that resounds with crowds, everything being equal. It turns into an all inclusive theme, a demonstration of the repeating idea of life and the unending pattern of birth, development, and reestablishment. In doing as such, the story perceives the social and verifiable aspects that raise the introduction of the primary tooth past an individual achievement to an image implanted in the shared perspective.

In the end passages of "Birth of the Primary Tooth," the story expects an intelligent tone, welcoming perusers to mull over the significant excursion implanted in this apparently little occasion. It urges them to perceive the complex transaction of science, feeling, culture, and history that merges in the rise of a youngster's most memorable tooth.

As perusers cross the account scene of "Birth of the Principal Tooth," they are not simple onlookers but rather dynamic members in a general story of development, love, and shared mankind. The principal tooth turns into an illustration for the murmurs of life, the complex dance of starting points and endings that shape the human experience.

It is a tribute to the verse tracked down in the standard, an investigation of the unprecedented inside the apparently ordinary snapshots of life. In praising the introduction of the main tooth, the account welcomes perusers to join the tune of mankind, recognizing the significant excellence that dwells in the patterns of life and the ageless dance of fresh starts.

1.2. The excitement and anticipation

In the delicate scene of youth, where every second is a material ready to be painted with the tints of revelation, the section named "The Energy and Expectation" spreads out like the petals of a sprouting bloom. A story catches the obvious energy and expectation that pervades the air as guardians anticipate the rise of a kid's most memorable tooth. This section is an orchestra of feelings, a fragile dance between trust, wonder, and the excitement of seeing an achievement that denotes the excursion from earliest stages to the baby years.

Whispers of Innocence

The excursion starts with the principal inconspicuous murmurs of getting teeth, those underlying suspicions that signal the looming appearance of a tooth. Guardians, gatekeepers, and relatives become sensitive to these unpretentious signals, becoming analysts in translating the quiet language of their baby's distress. The expanded slobber, the chewing on fingers or getting teeth toys, and an intermittent fastidiousness become the Morse code of expectation, flagging the approaching appearance of the principal tooth.

As the story unfurls, it catches the air inside the family, which changes into a safe house of assumption and energy. The simple notice of getting teeth summons a feeling of expectation that is both unmistakable and elusive. Parental figures wind up exploring this stage with a mix of energy and delicate trepidation, knowing that each slobber doused chin-wiper or therapeutic ring gripped in little fingers carries them one bit nearer to the noticeable rise of that first magnificent bud.

The expectation turns into a common encounter, an aggregate excursion that joins guardians, grandparents, and more distant family individuals in an embroidery of shared trust and delight. The air is accused of the implicit rush of seeing a second that proclaims the development and improvement of the youngster. It isn't just about the actual development of a tooth yet about the emblematic importance that this little occasion holds in the more extensive setting of the youngster's life.

The energy and expectation stretch out past the close family and into the mutual structure holding the system together. Companions, neighbors, and well-wishers become put resources into the unfurling account, anxious to partake in the delight of this achievement. The shared idea of the expectation mirrors the interconnectedness of human encounters, where the introduction of a youngster's most memorable tooth turns into a festival that rises above individual limits.

As parental figures anticipate the noticeable indications of getting teeth, there is a delicate dance between the known and the unexplored world. The energy is joined by a feeling of interest and miracle, as guardians consider the exceptional qualities that will characterize their kid's grin. Will it be the sparkling incisor that becomes the dominant focal point, or maybe a devilish canine that adds character to the smile? The expectation turns into an excursion of conceivable outcomes, a journey into the unknown domain of a youngster's arising dental scene.

In the tranquil snapshots of expectation, parental figures end up considering the progression of time. The main tooth turns into a substantial indication of the kid's development, a marker that depicts the change from the sticky grins of outset to the more complicated dental examples of toddlerhood. It is in this reflection that the energy takes on a self-contradicting connotation, as guardians wonder about the quick speed at which their youngster is developing.

The story then dives into the profound scene of expectation, investigating the nuanced feelings that go with the excursion. The energy is joined with a feeling of parental pride, an acknowledgment of the kid's versatility and the wonder of nature's plan. The main tooth turns into a declaration to the complex dance of hereditary qualities and science, a smaller than normal magnum opus that mirrors the novel personality of the kid.

All the while, there is an affirmation of the delicacy that goes with this stage. Getting teeth isn't just an actual cycle yet a common encounter that includes soothing the youngster through snapshots of distress. The expectation, touched with sympathy, turns into a delicate indication of the parental figure's job as a wellspring of comfort and backing during this momentary period.

The section then nimbly changes into the social components of fervor and expectation encompassing the primary tooth. Various societies and social orders have special customs and customs related with getting teeth, adding layers of significance to the overall account. Whether it be a stylized occasion, a unique dining experience, or the recognition of explicit traditions, the fervor takes on a social tint, mirroring the variety of human practices.

Moreover, the story investigates the job of fables and odd notions in molding the social impression of getting teeth. From the confidence in the influence of ornaments to safeguard the getting teeth kid to the thought that the planning of getting teeth can impact character qualities, these social subtleties improve the expectation with an embroidery of stories and convictions. It is a demonstration of the perplexing trap of social insight that encompasses the apparently basic demonstration of a tooth's rise.

As the story unfurls, it welcomes perusers to think about their own encounters of energy and expectation. The common widespread nature of these feelings turns into a scaffold that interfaces perusers across societies and ages. It is a challenge to return to the loved snapshots of hanging tight for a kid's most memorable tooth and to perceive the immortal magnificence implanted in the common human experience of nurturing.

The expectation isn't without its difficulties, and the account delicately investigates the normal obstacles looked by guardians during this stage. Restless evenings, getting teeth distress, and a periodic cantankerousness become essential strings in the texture of expectation. A depiction highlights the weakness of early stages and the strength expected of both kid and guardian during this period.

The story then, at that point, moves its concentration to the outside articulations of energy and expectation. Child showers, embellished with getting teeth toys and chin-wipers, become dynamic festivals that represent the aggregate expectation of the kid's most memorable tooth. It is a collective affirmation of the common excursion of being a parent, where loved ones hold hands in communicating their energy for the looming achievement.

As the primary indications of getting teeth become more articulated, the fervor heightens, arriving at a crescendo as the main tooth shows up. The story catches the euphoria that goes with this visual affirmation, a snapshot of win for both parent and youngster. It is in this disclosing that the expectation changes into a substantial reality, and the family is loaded up with a significant pride and bliss.

The fervor and expectation, in spite of the fact that arriving at its pinnacle with the development of the principal tooth, don't scatter yet advance into another stage. The story smoothly changes to investigate the continuous excursion of dental turn of events, perceiving that the principal tooth is only the underlying note in the orchestra of a youngster's developing grin. The expectation turns into a consistent string woven into the texture of life as a parent, an always present sidekick in the common encounters of development and improvement.

In the end sections, the story welcomes perusers to enjoy the magnificence tracked down in the normal snapshots of energy and expectation. It is a festival of the little delights that intersperse the excursion of being a parent, an acknowledgment that in the midst of the everyday practice of providing care, there are snapshots of enchantment and marvel. The principal tooth turns into a representation for the murmurs of delight and the limitless possible intrinsic in each phase of a kid's development.

As perusers navigate the story scene of "The Energy and Expectation," they are not latent eyewitnesses but rather dynamic members in a widespread story of trust, wonder, and shared humankind. The section welcomes them to embrace the immortal excellence implanted in the expectation of a kid's most memorable tooth, remembering it as a delicate sign of the unprecedented inside the customary, and a tribute to the getting through wizardry of being a parent.

In the proceeding with excursion of "The Fervor and Expectation," the story develops investigation of the profound subtleties go with the anticipated snapshot of the principal tooth's rise. It dives into the significant association between the guardian and the youngster, perceiving the expectation not only as an outside occasion but rather as a profoundly private and personal experience.

The fervor turns into its very own language, verbally expressed in the common looks between guardians, the quieted discussions between relatives, and the implicit comprehension that pervades the family. It is an aggregate heartbeat, resounding with the beat of shared expectations and dreams for the kid's future. The story welcomes perusers to feel the heartbeat of expectation, to detect the solidarity that emerges from a common vision of development and improvement.

As the story unfurls, it investigates the tactile scene of expectation — the delicate coos of the newborn child, the delicate murmur of cradlesongs, and the delicate strokes that convey consolation. The fervor isn't restricted to the noticeable; a vivid encounter draws in the faculties, making a rich embroidery of recollections that will be woven into the texture of family legend. A tribute to the tangible orchestra goes with the excursion toward the main tooth.

The section then, at that point, effortlessly advances to the public articulations of energy and expectation. Child showers, overflowing with giggling and embellished with getting teeth themed adornments, become dynamic services that represent the aggregate bliss and expectation of the kid's looming achievement. Loved ones, through their motions and gifts, become members in the common story, enhancing the fervor to an ensemble of festivity.

In investigating the social components of energy, the account reveals insight into the assorted manners by which various social orders express and ritualize this expectation. Whether it be the trading of conventional gifts, the recognition of customs went down through ages, or the making of social services, the part perceives the widespread string that meshes expectation into the texture of social character. It is an affirmation that the fervor encompassing a kid's most memorable tooth is an embroidery enhanced by the changed tones of worldwide practices.

The section doesn't avoid recognizing the difficulties that coincide with the fervor and expectation. The inconvenience of getting teeth, the restless evenings, and a periodic fastidiousness become indispensable pieces of the common experience. A depiction encourages compassion and fortitude, recognizing the weaknesses of both parent and kid during this momentary stage. The story stretches out a delicate hug to guardians, guaranteeing them that the difficulties are woven into the actual texture of the excursion and that they, as well, are essential for the common human experience of nurturing.

The story effortlessly finishes up by welcoming perusers to appreciate the excellence tracked down in the standard snapshots of fervor and expectation. It is a festival of the little victories, the common giggling, and the bonds reinforced by the excursion toward the primary tooth.

The section turns into an immortal reflection on the persevering through enchantment of life as a parent — an excursion checked by the development of actual achievements as well as by the murmurs of affection, delight, and shared expectation that reverberation through the passageways of youth. At these times, the standard changes into the uncommon, and the story turns into a challenge to savor the sorcery innate in the expectation of a youngster's most memorable tooth.

1.3. Parental reactions and celebrations

In the complicated embroidery of being a parent, the section named "Parental Responses and Festivities" unfurls as a significant investigation of the heap feelings that go with the appearance of a kid's most memorable tooth. A story dives into the profundities of parental happiness, the declarations of festivity that echo through families, and the one of a kind manners by which guardians answer this groundbreaking achievement.

The excursion starts with the uncovering of the main tooth, a second that fills in as an impetus for a variety of feelings inside guardians. The underlying response frequently includes a mix of shock, wonderment, and overpowering affection. Seeing that small, silvery bud getting through the gums is a visual demonstration of the youngster's development and improvement, and guardians wind up quickly suspended in a condition of marvel, wondering about the supernatural occurrence of life.

As the account unfurls, it explores through the range of parental responses, each as novel as the people encountering them. For some's purposes, the main bite denotes a substantial affirmation of their kid's advancement, summoning a feeling of achievement and pride. For other people, it turns into a close to home milestone, a piercing sign of the transient idea of earliest stages and the steady walk of time. The section embraces the variety of these responses, perceiving that the parental reaction to a youngster's most memorable tooth is a profoundly private and nuanced experience.

The parental festival of the main tooth stretches out past the close family, including the more extensive circle of family members and companions. Grandparents, specifically, assume a critical part in the celebrations, carrying with them an abundance of involvement and the point of view of ages. Their responses are frequently pervaded with sentimentality, as they draw matches between the rise of the primary tooth in the ongoing age and their own encounters as guardians.

The account then, at that point, effortlessly changes into the common part of festivities, where companions and more distant family individuals participate in the celebration. Child showers, enhanced with tooth-themed beautifications, become dynamic events that represent the aggregate happiness encompassing the youngster's formative achievement. It is a festival of the actual tooth as well as of the common excursion of nurturing, where the youngster turns into a point of convergence for aggregate fondness and festivity.

In investigating the social components of parental responses and festivities, the section enlightens the assorted manners by which various social orders express and ritualize this blissful event. From customary services to representative ceremonies, the parental reaction to the main tooth becomes joined with social practices that add profundity and significance to the overall story. It is an affirmation of the lavishness and variety of human customs that add to the festival of life's achievements.

Besides, the story looks at the job of legends and strange notions in molding the parental responses to the primary tooth. Social convictions encompassing the timing, appearance, and qualities of the main tooth add to the woven artwork of festivity. Whether it be the faith in the tooth's impact on future character attributes or the formal traditions related with its rise, these social subtleties add layers of importance to the parental reaction.

In the familial setting, the part investigates the transaction between parental responses and the kid's reaction to the festival. The youngster, frequently sensitive to the fervor and positive energy encompassing the principal tooth, ingests the delight like a wipe. The parental festival turns into a common encounter, encouraging a feeling of association and warmth inside the nuclear family. It is a demonstration of the corresponding idea of bliss, where the kid's enjoyment becomes interwoven with the parental festival.

The account doesn't avoid recognizing the difficulties that exist together with the festivals. Getting teeth distress, restless evenings, and a periodic particularity become fundamental pieces of this common experience. The parental reaction reaches out past simple festival to include a sustaining job, giving solace and backing to the kid during snapshots of getting teeth related distress. A depiction exemplifies the diverse idea of nurturing, where euphoria and difficulties blend in a fragile dance.

As the account unfurls, it welcomes perusers to think about their own encounters of parental responses and festivities. The common widespread nature of these feelings turns into a scaffold that interfaces perusers across societies and ages. It is a challenge to return to the esteemed snapshots of commending a youngster's most memorable tooth, perceiving the immortal magnificence implanted in the common human experience of nurturing.

The part effortlessly finishes up by featuring the persevering through effect of parental responses and festivities on the familial account. The primary tooth turns out to be in excess of an actual achievement; it turns into an image of the adoration, happiness, and shared encounters that characterize the parent-kid relationship. The festivals, whether fabulous or cozy, leave a permanent engraving on the family's aggregate memory, making a supply of loved minutes that will be returned to with affection in the years to come.

As perusers cross the account scene of "Parental Responses and Festivities," they are not detached spectators but rather dynamic members in a widespread story of adoration, bliss, and shared mankind. The part turns into a tribute to the persevering through wizardry implanted in the parental reaction to a youngster's most memorable tooth, remembering it as a demonstration of the phenomenal inside the conventional, and a confirmation of the significant excellence tracked down in the common excursion of being a parent.

In the proceeded with investigation of "Parental Responses and Festivities," the story dives further into the profound propensities that describe the parental reaction to a youngster's most memorable tooth. It examines the complicated interchange of feelings, going from the underlying astonishment and marvel to the persevering through deep satisfaction and happiness that goes with this achievement.

The disclosing of the primary tooth turns into an impactful second that embodies the quintessence of life as a parent. A disclosure rises above the actual development of a tooth; it represents the guardians' job as stewards of a striking excursion. The part highlights that the parental reaction isn't simply a response to an organic occasion yet an affirmation of the consecrated liability shared with guardians — the supporting of new life and the development of a flourishing, versatile person.

As the story unfurls, it features the different range of parental responses, each affected by the interesting characters, encounters, and viewpoints of individual guardians. A few guardians might get themselves awestruck by the sheer wonder of seeing a small tooth getting through the gums, while others might be cleared away by a flood of sentimentality, thinking back about the beginning of earliest stages. The section embraces this variety, perceiving that the parental reaction to a kid's most memorable tooth is a material painted with the heap shades of individual experience.

Parental festivals stretch out past the close family circle, making waves of happiness that contact grandparents, aunties, uncles, and dear companions. Grandparents, specifically, frequently assume an exceptional part in these festivals. Their responses are implanted with the insight borne of involvement, as they draw matches between the primary tooth of the ongoing age and that of their own kids. Their cooperation in the festival turns into a scaffold between ages, connecting the past, present, and future in a common embroidery of familial happiness.

In looking at the public part of festivities, the account amplifies the meaning of child showers and get-togethers. These become a bigger number of than simple celebrations; they change into ceremonies that represent the aggregate hug of a developing family. Companions and more distant family individuals add to the festival, transforming it into a common story where the kid turns into a point of convergence for aggregate warmth and shared delight. The section catches the pith of these shared festivals as lively articulations of the interconnectedness of connections.

The social elements of parental responses and festivities are additionally enlightened, highlighting the manners by which various social orders express and ritualize this upbeat event. The section perceives that social practices and convictions add layers of significance to the parental reaction, advancing the festival with the embroidered artwork of worldwide customs. It turns into an investigation of the widespread and various strings that mesh into the texture of life as a parent, making the festival of a kid's most memorable tooth a multifaceted peculiarity.

Besides, the account develops its investigation of fables and odd notions, revealing insight into the social subtleties that impact parental responses. Whether it be the faith in the defensive influence of a talisman or the adherence to explicit traditions, these social components add to the extravagance of the festival. The parental reaction turns into a dance among custom and contemporary experience, a combination that mirrors the developing idea of social personality.

The familial setting is returned to with an emphasis on the interaction between parental responses and the youngster's reaction to the festival. The kid, on top of the profound energy encompassing the primary tooth, turns into a functioning member in the common experience. The parental festival turns into a common happiness, encouraging a feeling of association and warmth inside the nuclear family. A festival stretches out past the actual development of the tooth, embracing the profound bonds that characterize the parent-youngster relationship.

Recognizing the difficulties that go with the festival, the story underscores the strength expected of guardians during the getting teeth stage. The parental reaction stretches out past the celebration to include a sustaining job, giving solace and backing to the youngster during snapshots of getting teeth related uneasiness. A depiction typifies the multi-layered nature of nurturing, where euphoria and difficulties mix in a sensitive dance.

The part smoothly finishes up by highlighting the persevering through effect of parental responses and festivities on the familial story. The primary tooth turns into an image of actual development as well as of the adoration, satisfaction, and shared encounters that characterize the parent-kid relationship. The festivals, whether fantastic or private, leave a permanent engraving on the family's aggregate memory, making a repository of loved minutes that become a necessary piece of the family's story embroidery.

As perusers cross the story scene of "Parental Responses and Festivities," they are not uninvolved spectators but rather dynamic members in a widespread story of adoration, happiness, and shared mankind. The section turns into a tribute to the getting through enchantment implanted in the parental reaction to a kid's most memorable tooth, remembering it as a demonstration of the remarkable inside the normal, and a certification of the significant excellence tracked down in the common excursion of life as a parent.

Chapter 2

Tiny Teeth, Big Dreams

Minuscule Teeth, Large Dreams: A Narrative of Experience growing up's Starting points

In the charming embroidery of youth, a part unfurls, decorated with the title "Little Teeth, Enormous Dreams." This story is a lovely investigation of the wondrous excursion that starts with the rise of those microscopic yet significant markers of development — minuscule teeth. An excursion rises above the physiological parts of dental turn of events, digging into the fantasies, expectations, and goals that mesh themselves into the texture of a youngster's incipient presence.

The story starts with the unpretentious messengers of getting teeth, the murmurs of small teeth planning to make their introduction. Guardians, sensitive to the subtleties of their youngster's signs, become spectators of these fragile prefaces — the expanded slobber, the delicate biting on fingers or getting teeth toys, and an intermittent fretfulness. These signs, much the same as the delicate notes of an introduction, predict the impending appearance of small teeth, establishing the groundwork for an ensemble of development.

As the main tooth gets through the gums, the story blossoms into a festival of the supernatural. It isn't simply a physiological event however a significant achievement that proclaims the origin of a kid's fantasies. The rise of small teeth turns into a material whereupon the imaginativeness of a youngster's future is portrayed, a figurative dawn that enlightens the huge scene of potential outcomes that anticipate.

The substance of "Minuscule Teeth, Enormous Dreams" lies in the actual sign of teeth as well as in the representative reverberation they hold. These small polish buds become diplomats of the youngster's prospering character, the planners of the brilliant grins that will charm hearts and the apparatuses with which they will explore the world. A story welcomes perusers to consider the uncommon likely epitomized inside these modest dental fortunes.

The section then effortlessly advances into the exchange of dreams and reality, investigating the job of creative mind and desire in the realm of life as a youngster. Minuscule teeth, similar to watchman sentinels, stand observer to the kaleidoscope of dreams that flash in the personalities of youngsters. From unconventional goals of becoming space travelers or princesses to the sincere fantasies about becoming specialists or firemen, every tooth turns into a quiet partner to the desires that unfurl in the fruitful soil of a youngster's creative mind.

As the account unfurls, it digs into the harmonious connection between the physical and powerful parts of experience growing up. The development of minuscule teeth becomes entwined with the development of dreams, framing a consistent continuum. The part welcomes perusers to think about the fragile dance between the substantial achievements of dental turn of events and the immaterial, ethereal nature of life as a youngster dreams.

The account then embraces the mutual part of young life dreams, perceiving that they are not singular substances but rather strings woven into the aggregate embroidery of familial and cultural assumptions. Guardians, grandparents, and parental figures add to the story of a kid's fantasies, engraving their own expectations and dreams onto the material of the youngster's expanding cognizance. It is a common excursion, where small teeth become the quiet observers to the mixture of familial and cultural yearnings.

In investigating the social components of "Little Teeth, Large Dreams," the account uncovers the assorted manners by which various social orders express and sustain youth desires. Whether it be through social transitional experiences, customary functions, or narrating, the section perceives that fantasies are individual pursuits as well as social inheritances went down through ages. Small teeth, in this unique circumstance, become vessels conveying the aggregate insight and goals of a local area.

Moreover, the account smoothly explores through the difficulties that go with the sensitive dance of dreams and reality. The inescapable tempests of frustration, an intermittent diversions, and the flexibility expected to explore the exciting bends in the road of life become essential features of the excursion. It is an affirmation that the street from small teeth to huge dreams isn't generally smooth however one that winds around the embroidered artwork of character and determination.

As the part unfurls, it ponders the convergence of training and goals, perceiving the significant job of learning in supporting enormous dreams. The school years, set apart by the shedding of child teeth and the development of long-lasting ones, become a pot for the refinement and development of experience growing up dreams. It is an extraordinary period where the underlying murmurs of yearning develop into additional characterized shapes, directed by the supporting hands of instructors, tutors, and parental figures.

The story then, at that point, welcomes perusers to look into the universe of sleep time stories, where the sorcery of narrating turns into an impetus for the blooming of enormous dreams. From fantasies that light the flash of creative mind to tales that bestow moral examples, every story adds to the rich soil in which dreams flourish. Little teeth, in their quiet rest, become observers to the nighttime orchestra of dreams taking off.

The familial setting is returned to with an emphasis on the transaction between parental direction and youth dreams. Guardians, with their exceptional mix of intelligence and love, become stewards of their kid's desires. The story enlightens the sensitive harmony between sustaining dreams and permitting the kid the independence to investigate and characterize their own way. It is a dance of direction and opportunity, where little teeth stand as unfaltering sidekicks in the excursion of self-disclosure.

In crossing the scene of "Little Teeth, Huge Dreams," the account considers the change from youth to puberty. The shedding of child teeth, joined by the development of extremely durable ones, turns into an illustration for the developing idea of dreams. The fantasies that once grown in the prolific soil of life as a youngster presently take on additional characterized shapes, impacted by the changing scene of youth. It is an impactful snapshot of transformation, where the reverberations of experience growing up dreams mix with the prospering yearnings of pre-adulthood.

The section effortlessly finishes up by welcoming perusers to enjoy the ageless excellence tracked down in the association of little teeth and large dreams. It is an investigation of the remarkable expected exemplified inside the conventional snapshots of young life.

The account turns into a tribute to the significant excursion from the development of small teeth, proclaiming the appearance of dreams, to the broad skylines of enormous dreams that unfurl as youngsters venture towards adulthood. In this investigation, perusers are not simple onlookers but rather dynamic members in the widespread orchestra of development, creative mind, and the persevering through wizardry of life as a youngster dreams.

The proceeded with investigation of "Little Teeth, Large Dreams" dives further into the complexities of life as a youngster's excursion, winding around a story that unfurls like an embroidery of dreams and desires. As little teeth show up, they become actual markers of development as well as allegories for the extensive dreams that flourish in the prolific soil of experience growing up.

The story further explores the interaction between the substantial truth of dental turn of events and the immaterial, ethereal domain of dreams. Small teeth, arising like pearls in a kid's grin, stand as quiet sentinels to the fantasies that flash in the openings of the youthful psyche. It is a cooperative relationship, where the actual development of teeth becomes interwoven with the development of dreams, making an amicable dance between the substantial and the immaterial.

Youth dreams, as the story explains, are not singular elements but rather strings unpredictably woven into the aggregate embroidery of familial and cultural assumptions. The impact of guardians, grandparents, and parental figures turns into a molding force, engraving the youngster's expanding cognizance with a mosaic of expectations and dreams. The fantasies, similar to ringlets connecting, become piece of a common story, a mutual excursion where little teeth demonstrate the veracity of the mixture of familial and cultural yearnings.

In investigating the social components of "Little Teeth, Enormous Dreams," the account spreads out the bunch manners by which various social orders express and support adolescence goals. Social transitional experiences, conventional services, and the rich embroidered artwork of narrating customs become channels through which dreams are sent across ages. The section perceives that fantasies are individual pursuits as well as social inheritances went down through the ages, and little teeth become vessels conveying the aggregate insight and desires of a local area.

The excursion from little teeth to enormous dreams, the story reflects, is certainly not a straight direction however a wandering way loaded with difficulties and wins. The tempests of dissatisfaction, an intermittent diversions, and the strength expected to explore the exciting bends in the road of life become essential aspects of the story. It is an affirmation that the street from little teeth to enormous dreams isn't generally smooth yet one that winds around the woven artwork of character, strength, and the unstoppable soul of versatility.

Schooling arises as a crucial section in the story, an extraordinary period where dreams are refined, and desires take on additional characterized shapes. The shedding of child teeth and the rise of long-lasting ones line up with the development of dreams, directed by the sustaining hands of instructors, coaches, and parental figures. The story thinks about the job of learning in molding large dreams, changing the murmurs of experience growing up desires into additional explained and deliberate dreams.

Sleep time stories, as the account unfurls, become captivated entrances through which the wizardry of narrating sustains the seeds of enormous dreams. Fantasies that flash the creative mind, tales that confer moral illustrations, and the rich story embroidered artwork of sleep time become essential components in the improvement of dreams. Small teeth, settled in the calm of the evening, demonstrate the veracity of the nighttime orchestra of dreams taking off, enlightened by the delicate gleam of narrating.

The familial setting is returned to with an accentuation on the sensitive dance between parental direction and the independence for a youngster to investigate and characterize their own way. Guardians, with their extraordinary mix of insight and love, become stewards of their youngster's goals. The account enlightens the mind boggling balance between sustaining dreams and permitting the kid the opportunity to find their own interests. It is a dance of direction and freedom, where small teeth stand as undaunted sidekicks in the excursion of self-revelation.

As the story proceeds, it mulls over the progress from youth to pre-adulthood — a period set apart by the shedding of child teeth and the development of long-lasting ones. This change turns into a representation for the developing idea of dreams. The fantasies that once grown in the ripe soil of life as a youngster presently take on additional characterized shapes, impacted by the changing scene of youth. It is a strong snapshot of transformation, where the reverberations of life as a youngster dreams mix with the expanding desires of puberty, and minuscule teeth become observers to the effortless change.

The part smoothly closes by welcoming perusers to relish the ageless excellence tracked down in the association of little teeth and large dreams. It is an investigation of the remarkable likely typified inside the customary snapshots of experience growing up. The account turns into a tribute to the significant excursion from the development of minuscule teeth, proclaiming the appearance of dreams, to the sweeping skylines of huge dreams that unfurl as kids venture towards adulthood. In this investigation, perusers are not simple onlookers but rather dynamic members in the general orchestra of development, creative mind, and the getting through enchantment of experience growing up dreams.

As perusers cross the story scene of "Minuscule Teeth, Huge Dreams," they are coaxed into an existence where the particulars of dental improvement combines with the unfathomable spread of young life dreams. An odyssey welcomes examination on the complex dance between the substantial and the elusive, the public and the individual, and the customary and the remarkable.

In the embroidery of little teeth and enormous dreams, the story turns into an immortal reflection on the charming excursion of young life — an excursion set apart by the murmurs of development, the kaleidoscope of desires, and the getting through enchantment of dreams that enlighten the way towards a brilliant future.

2.1. The Toddler's World

The Baby's Reality: An Ensemble of Disclosure

In the delicate domain of youth, the section named "The Baby's Reality" spreads out as a lively embroidery, catching the embodiment of a period set apart by limitless interest, unrestrained investigation, and the orchestra of revelation. A story wanders into the complexities of toddlerhood, where each second turns into a material painted with the tints of learning and the enchantment of new encounters.

The excursion starts with an investigation of the physical and mental achievements that describe the little child years. The story digs into the blooming portability of babies, those first speculative advances that envoy a recently discovered freedom. The world, once saw from the vantage reason behind creeping or cruising, grows dramatically as little children explore their environmental factors with a blend of assurance and flimsy beauty. The rise of language, set apart by the captivating jibber jabber and the principal recognizable words, adds a melodic layer to the ensemble of improvement.

As the account unfurls, it welcomes perusers to look into the kaleidoscope of feelings that characterize the baby's reality. Fits of rage and tears, chuckling and happiness — all become basic notes in the orchestra of toddlerhood. The part investigates the close to home scene of this period, perceiving that little children are exploring a reality where their thriving independence crashes into a blossoming need for security and consolation. It is a fragile dance of feelings, a story that unfurls with the delicacy expected to grasp the intricacies of the little child's heart.

The baby's reality is a scene of investigation, and the story turns into a vivid excursion into the domains of play and revelation. From the sorcery of a first experience with building blocks to the tactile enjoyment of finger painting, each experience turns into a venturing stone in the little child's odyssey of learning. The section unfurls as a festival of play — a principal language through which little children interpret their general surroundings, express inventiveness, and fashion associations with both their environmental factors and their prospering identity.

In analyzing the mental elements of the baby's reality, the account nimbly explores through the charming domain of creative mind. Regular items become gateways to fantastical undertakings, and the normal changes into the exceptional according to a little child. The story welcomes perusers to observe the blooming innovativeness of babies, as they summon fictional universes and weave stories with the straightforwardness and enchantment that main youth can typify.

The part then, at that point, delicately changes into the job of guardians in forming and sustaining the baby's reality. Guardians, gatekeepers, and teachers become stewards of this developmental period, giving a protected framework to the baby's investigation and revelation. The story investigates the fragile harmony between encouraging freedom and giving direction — a dance that requires both responsiveness and trust. Parental figures become orchestrators of the little child's ensemble, directing their means while permitting the tune of disclosure to naturally unfurl.

As the story unfurls, it thinks about the job of language securing in the baby's reality. The rise of words and the advancement of relational abilities become vital achievements, opening new channels for articulation and association. The part turns into a reflection on the captivating system of language improvement, where each expressed word turns into a scaffold between the baby and the more extensive world.

In investigating the social components of the little child's reality, the story focuses a light on the blooming connections that structure the groundwork of early socialization. From the main fellowships fashioned in playgroups to the delicate bonds with relatives, the little child's reality reaches out past individual investigation to incorporate the glow of social associations. A story highlights the meaning of connections in forming the close to home scene of toddlerhood.

The part nimbly dives into the tactile encounters that characterize the baby's reality. The material delight of crunching mud between minuscule fingers, the olfactory joy of investigating different fragrances, and the visual dining experience of dynamic varieties all add to the ensemble of tactile revelation. The story turns into a sensorial excursion, recognizing the significant effect of tangible encounters in laying the foundation for mental and profound turn of events.

In crossing the scene of "The Baby's Reality," the account considers the difficulties that coincide with the delights of revelation. The mission for freedom, albeit a sign of toddlerhood, isn't without its obstacles. The account explores the fragile dance between affirming independence and looking for solace from guardians. It turns into an investigation of the equilibrium expected to help a baby's developing freedom while giving the security they need to explore the intricacies of the world.

The familial setting is returned to with an accentuation on the job of the nuclear family in molding the baby's reality. Kin elements, the impact of more distant family, and the aggregate encounters shared inside the family become fundamental components in the account. The part turns into a tribute to the significance of family as the foundation of a little child's initial encounters, a steady design that cultivates development, love, and a feeling of having a place.

As the story proceeds, the account considers the changes inside the little child's reality — the steady advancement from the early baby a very long time to the limit of preschool. It ponders the mixed idea of this period, where the little child's reality grows past the natural limits of home to incorporate the more extensive local area. The story turns into a strong investigation of development, recognizing that each step in the right direction conveys with it the reverberations of the little child's prior orchestra of revelation.

The part nimbly finishes up by welcoming perusers to enjoy the ageless magnificence tracked down in the multifaceted woven artwork of "The Baby's Reality." It is an investigation of the phenomenal likely epitomized inside the normal snapshots of youth. The story turns into a tribute to the significant excursion from those conditional initial steps to the sure walks of preschool status — an excursion set apart by the murmurs of development, the kaleidoscope of feelings, and the persevering through enchantment of revelation that enlightens the way towards a brilliant future.

In navigating the story scene of "The Baby's Reality," perusers are not simple observers but rather dynamic members in the widespread ensemble of youth — an orchestra that resounds with the giggling of play, the tune of language, and the concordance of close to home investigation. The part turns into a reverence to the fragile dance of toddlerhood, an affirmation of the captivating existence where each revelation, each stagger, and each common second adds to the ageless mood of development, interest, and the getting through enchantment of the little child's reality.

Proceeding with the investigation of "The Baby's Reality," the story plummets further into the complex subtleties of this enamoring time of youth. It spreads out as a multi-layered embroidery, winding around together the strings of interest, feeling, and disclosure that characterize the little child's reality.

In diving further into the profound scene of toddlerhood, the account enlightens the vital job of feelings in molding the baby's encounters. The ensemble of giggling, tears, and the unfathomable energy that portrays this stage turns into a rich range through which little children express their prospering identity. The part turns into a melodious investigation of the profound crescendos and diminuendos that intersperse the baby's reality — an existence where the declaration of sentiments is both over the top and true.

As the story unfurls, it examines the intriguing domain of pretend inside the little child's reality. The mystical transaction of creative mind and reality turns into a focal subject, where regular items change into fantastical curios, and conventional spaces transform into captivated domains. The section turns into a demonstration of the innate inventiveness of babies, as they explore the liquid limits between the unmistakable and the nonexistent, building stories that mirror the marvel of their developing personalities.

The investigation of play inside the baby's reality becomes the overwhelming focus, and the story turns into a festival of the bunch manners by which little children draw in with their current circumstance. From single snapshots of centered play to the cooperative energy of playdates, every communication turns into a brushstroke in the magnum opus of toddlerhood. The part explores through the perky scenes of sandboxes, jungle gyms, and parlors — the fields where the sorcery of revelation unfurls.

In analyzing the mental components of the little child's reality, the account nimbly changes into the domain of critical thinking and direction. Ordinary difficulties, from stacking blocks to arranging shapes, become open doors for mental development. The section turns into an investigation of the little child's prospering skills to break down, plan, and get a handle on the world — a cycle that unfurls with a brilliant mix of assurance and quiltlessness.

As the story unfurls, it welcomes perusers to observe the advancement of language inside the little child's reality. The primary unmistakable words and the charming chatter become vital notes in the orchestra of correspondence. The part turns into a reflection on the extraordinary force of language, a device that empowers babies to communicate their necessities as well as fills in as an extension to interface with individuals around them. It is an excursion through the rich scene of phonetic turn of events, where each word turns into a venturing stone toward a more unpredictable embroidery of correspondence.

The story smoothly wanders through the social elements of the little child's reality, revealing insight into the significance of connections and social cooperations. From the elements of playdates to the delicate bonds fashioned with parental figures, the section unfurls as a recognition for the meaning of association in molding the baby's close to home scene. An investigation of the social subtleties add to the embroidery of early connections, cultivating a feeling of having a place and shared encounters.

In thinking about the difficulties inside the little child's reality, the account dives into the landscape of advances. The move from the case of home to the more extensive local area of preschool denotes a crucial crossroads in the baby's excursion. The section turns into a reflection on the versatile strength expected to explore new conditions, new faces, and the growing skylines of social commitment. It recognizes that each change conveys with it the reverberations of the little child's previous orchestra, an amicable mix of commonality and oddity.

The familial setting is returned to with an accentuation on the continuous job of families in supporting and sustaining the baby's reality. Guardians and parental figures stay resolute colleagues in this odyssey, giving direction, solace, and a protected starting point for investigation. The part turns into an affirmation of the getting through meaning of the nuclear family — a steady in the midst of the consistently changing scenes of toddlerhood.

As the account effortlessly closes, it stretches out a solicitation to perusers to ponder the persevering through wizardry tracked down in the ensemble of "The Baby's Reality." It is an investigation of the uncommon possible typified inside the conventional snapshots of youth. The part turns into an immortal tribute to the significant excursion from conditional initial steps to the certain steps of preschool preparation — an excursion set apart by the murmurs of development, the kaleidoscope of feelings, and the persevering through enchantment of revelation that enlightens the way towards a brilliant future.

In navigating the story scene of "The Baby's Reality," perusers are not simple observers but rather dynamic members in the widespread orchestra of youth — an ensemble that resounds with the chuckling of play, the song of language, and the congruity of profound investigation. The part turns into a tribute to the sensitive dance of toddlerhood, an affirmation of the captivating existence where each disclosure, each stagger, and each common second adds to the immortal musicality of development, interest, and the getting through wizardry of the baby's reality.

2.2. Exploring the early years of childhood

Investigating the Early Long stretches of Life as a youngster: An Excursion of Revelation

In the rich embroidery of human life, the early long stretches of life as a youngster arise as a multicolored display, a material painted with the shades of development, disclosure, and limitless potential. This story leaves on an investigation of this extraordinary period, digging into the multifaceted embroidery of encounters that shape the underpinning of an individual's life. An excursion rises above the limits of time, culture, and individual contrasts, winding around together the widespread strings that characterize the pith of youth.

The odyssey begins with an examination of the physiological and mental achievements that mark the early years. From the primary breaths of outset to the provisional strides of toddlerhood, each formative stage turns into a section in the unfurling story of youth. The story investigates the marvels of engine expertise improvement, the blooming of mental capacities, and the ensemble of profound development that moves through these early stages.

As the account unfurls, it welcomes perusers to look into the universe of tactile investigation that describes youth. The material joy of feeling various surfaces, the olfactory extravagance of new aromas, and the visual gala of energetic varieties become doors to understanding and collaborating with the world. The part turns into an inundation into the sensorial orchestra that shapes the early encounters of life as a youngster, where each touch, smell, and sight adds to the distinctive mosaic of discernment.

In pondering the profound scene of youth, the story explores through the delicate intricacies of feelings and connections. The primary grins of acknowledgment, the glow of familial bonds, and a periodic tears of dissatisfaction or euphoria become essential notes in the close to home ensemble of youth. An investigation of the primary connections give the profound platform to a youngster's prospering identity.

The story smoothly changes into the domain of language procurement, where the seeds of correspondence flourish and sprout. The chattering of babies develops into the captivating tunes of first words, flagging the rise of a youngster's capacity to offer viewpoints and sentiments. The section turns into a reflection on the groundbreaking force of language, an instrument that works with correspondence as well as fills in as a course for the improvement of mental and interactive abilities.

The investigation of youth stretches out past the individual, embracing the familial setting as a crucial background. Guardians, parental figures, and more distant family individuals become dynamic members in the story, adding to the sustaining and forming of a kid's initial years. The section turns into a tribute to the job of families as the bedrock of help, love, and direction during this primary period. It dives into the fragile dance between encouraging freedom and giving a protected close to home anchor — a dance that requires both responsiveness and trust.

As the story unfurls, it considers the charming universe of play inside the scene of youth. Play turns into the language through which kids unravel the complexities of their environmental factors, express imagination, and fashion associations with both their friends and the advancing self. The section turns into an investigation of the different types of play — from inventive pretending to organized games — that add to the all encompassing improvement of a kid.

In navigating the scene of youth, the story effortlessly investigates the meaning of social impacts and cultural settings. It dives into the manners by which social convictions, customs, and cultural assumptions shape the early encounters of kids. The section turns into an affirmation of the variety intrinsic in the worldwide embroidery of youth, where social subtleties add layers of importance to the widespread excursion of development and revelation.

The investigation stretches out into the instructive domain, pondering the job of youth schooling in forming the direction of learning. From the organized conditions of preschools to the casual environments of locally established learning, the story turns into a reflection on the diverse scenes of early schooling. It investigates the manners by which early growth opportunities lay the foundation for mental, social, and profound turn of events, making way for a long lasting excursion of interest and request.

As the story proceeds, the account ponders the changes inside the early years — the shift from the casing of home to the more extensive skylines of formal tutoring. It explores the difficulties and energies that go with this change, remembering it as a critical point in the continuous story of young life. The part turns into a reflection on the versatile flexibility expected to explore new conditions, new connections, and the growing skylines of information.

The familial setting is returned to with an accentuation on the advancing jobs of guardians and parental figures as kids change through the early years. The account turns into an investigation of the unique interchange among freedom and direction, recognizing that the requirements of youngsters develop as they explore the changing scenes of development. It is a demonstration of the persevering through connection among guardians and youngsters — a bond that adjusts and changes as the story of youth unfurls.

In considering the difficulties inside the early long stretches of life as a youngster, the story dives into the territory of individual contrasts and remarkable formative directions. It recognizes that every youngster is a particular element, with their own speed of development, qualities, and areas of challenge. The part turns into an investigation of the significance of perceiving and regarding the variety innate in the youth account, encouraging a comprehensive and strong climate for each kid.

The investigation of youth effortlessly finishes up by welcoming perusers to appreciate the immortal magnificence tracked down in the complex embroidery of development and disclosure. It is an investigation of the uncommon possible exemplified inside the common snapshots of youth. The story turns into an immortal tribute to the significant excursion from the support of outset to the edge of formal instruction — an excursion set apart by the murmurs of development, the kaleidoscope of feelings, and the persevering through wizardry of revelation that enlightens the way towards a brilliant future.

In crossing the account scene of "Investigating the Early Long periods of Life as a youngster," perusers are not simple observers but rather dynamic members in the general orchestra of development, interest, and the getting through sorcery of youth. The part turns into a tribute to the sensitive dance of revelation, an affirmation of the captivating reality where each achievement, each inclination, and each common second adds to the immortal cadence of human turn of events.

2.3. Symbolism of milk teeth in innocence
The Imagery of Milk Teeth: Watchmen of Honesty

In the complex embroidery of human life, imagery meshes strings of importance into the texture of our lives, saturating ordinary articles with importance that rises above the commonplace. Among these, the imagery of milk teeth arises as a powerful and widespread representation, filling in as watchmen of blamelessness in the excursion from youth to pre-adulthood.

At the actual center of this imagery lies the physiological change of child teeth, otherwise called deciduous or milk teeth. These small pearls, settled inside the mouths of newborn children, represent the underlying phases of development and improvement. The shedding of these milk teeth turns into an unmistakable marker of the progression of time, a visual demonstration of the recurrent idea of life. As these teeth fall away, accounting for the development of super durable ones, they represent the progress from the cover of youth to the more perplexing scene of pre-adulthood.

The guiltlessness epitomized in milk teeth is significant, addressing a phase of life immaculate by the intricacies and difficulties that anticipate not too far off. In their perfect whiteness and small size, milk teeth summon a feeling of immaculateness and weakness. They are a material whereupon the underlying strokes of life's encounters are painted — a material that, briefly, stays immaculate by the more extensive strokes of the world's intricacies.

The imagery of milk teeth flourishes in social accounts, old stories, and antiquated customs. In many societies, the shedding of milk teeth is joined by ceremonies and customs that commend the youngster's progress into another period of life. The tooth pixie, a capricious figure in Western fables, is one such model. In this practice, youngsters place their lost milk teeth under their pads around evening time, and the tooth pixie trades them for a little prize, denoting a fun loving affirmation of the kid's development.

In addition, the imagery of milk teeth reaches out past the individual and into the shared awareness of social orders. In writing, workmanship, and film, milk teeth frequently act as powerful images of immaculateness, weakness, and the brief idea of experience growing up. They become story gadgets that summon a feeling of wistfulness and reflection on the fleetingness of youth.

The story unfurls further as we ponder the physiological parts of milk teeth. These deciduous teeth, framing the underlying set in a human's dentition, are placeholders for the long-lasting dentition that will follow. The shedding of milk teeth is a characteristic and consecutive interaction, reflecting the recurrent idea of life. In this natural transformation, there is a lovely reverberation — the old clearing a path for the new, the impermanent respecting the long-lasting.

The imagery of milk teeth likewise stretches out into the domain of language and correspondence. The rise of a kid's most memorable teeth, the milk teeth, is in many cases joined by the improvement of language abilities. The chattering of babies develops into the explanation of first words, denoting a critical stage in the kid's excursion toward self-articulation. The imagery here is layered, proposing that the immaculateness of early correspondence, untainted by the intricacies of grown-up talk, tracks down its lined up in the perfect whiteness of milk teeth.

Besides, the honesty typified in milk teeth is entwined with the subjects of trust and reliance. In the early long stretches of life as a youngster, a kid's confidence in their parental figures is unfaltering. The dependence on guardians or gatekeepers for food, care, and direction is reflected in the dependence on milk teeth for the underlying phases of biting and sustenance. The imagery lies in this harmonious relationship — a relationship established in trust and weakness.

As the account unfurls, it considers the social and cultural assumptions related with the imagery of milk teeth. The deficiency of the primary milk tooth is in many cases seen as a soul changing experience, flagging the youngster's status for additional critical obligations and difficulties. The imagery reaches out past the singular experience to envelop the aggregate assumptions implanted in the social texture. It turns into a common story — an all inclusive affirmation of the certainty of development and change.

In investigating the imagery of milk teeth, the story dives into the profound reverberation of this similitude. The shedding of milk teeth, frequently joined by a blend of energy and dread, denotes an unmistakable step towards development. The imagery typifies the impactful magnificence of advances — the sensitive harmony between clutching the solace of life as a youngster and embracing the vulnerabilities of pre-adulthood. It turns into an image of flexibility, versatility, and the inborn limit of people to explore the consistently changing flows of life.

In addition, the imagery of milk teeth is unpredictably associated with the idea of misfortune and fleetingness. The shedding of child teeth is a substantial sign of the fleetingness inborn in the human experience. It fills in as a microcosm of the more extensive subject of fleetingness — the recurrent idea of life where each misfortune makes ready for fresh starts. In this imagery, there is an intrinsic insight, welcoming consideration on the ephemerality of youth and the certainty of progress.

As the account proceeds, it investigates the profound scene encompassing the idea of the tooth pixie. Past its energetic and capricious nature, the tooth pixie custom turns into a social articulation of parental consideration and support.

The little prize left by the tooth pixie fills in as an unmistakable affirmation of the kid's mental fortitude in confronting the vulnerabilities of progress. A ceremonial scaffolds the fanciful with the genuine, making a space for youngsters to explore the close to home intricacies of growing up.

The imagery of milk teeth additionally tracks down reverberation in the more extensive setting of cultural assumptions and social stories. In certain societies, the lost milk teeth are saved or discarded in unambiguous customs, crediting magical or defensive characteristics to these little leftovers. The social importance lies in the conviction that the substance of blamelessness epitomized in the milk teeth can act as a charm against mischief or mishap.

Moreover, the story ponders the emblematic associations between milk teeth and personality. The rise of extremely durable teeth means actual development as well as a more profound investigation of selfhood. The imagery lies in the possibility that as the youngster sheds the last remnants of youth, they step into a more nuanced comprehension of their personality. The milk teeth become markers of a former time, nostalgic tokens of the straightforwardness and virtue that describe the early years.

In looking at the imagery of milk teeth, the story returns to the social and cultural aspects, recognizing that these images are not static yet develop across time and across various networks. The liquid idea of imagery is reflected in the different ways in which societies decipher and praise the shedding of milk teeth. The account turns into an investigation of the rich embroidered artwork of convictions and works on, highlighting the widespread topics of development, change, and the strength of the human soul.

In addition, the imagery of milk teeth welcomes reflection on the job of guardians in directing kids through these changes. The story unfurls as an affirmation of the fragile dance between clutching the remainders of young life and empowering the kid to step into the unknown region of puberty. Guardians become stewards of this emblematic excursion, offering both the help expected to explore change and the space for the kid to attest their arising character.

The story smoothly closes by welcoming perusers to ponder the getting through imagery of milk teeth — an imagery that rises above social and worldly limits. It is an investigation of the widespread topics woven into the texture of this similitude — subjects of honesty, strength, misfortune, and the never-ending pattern of development and change. The milk teeth, in their transitory presence, become watchmen of an immortal story — one that unfurls in the hearts of youngsters, guardians, and social orders the same.

The Imagery of Milk Teeth: Blamelessness Epitomized

In the immense spread of human experience, imagery fills in as a strong language, permitting us to permeate standard items with significant importance. Among these images, milk teeth stand as quiet watchmen of honesty, conveying with them the heaviness of young life's momentary virtue. Inside the small edges and fragile underlying foundations of these deciduous teeth lies a figurative profundity that rises above their physiological capability.

At its embodiment, the imagery of milk teeth tracks down its underlying foundations in the physiological excursion from early stages to immaturity. These little teeth, otherwise called deciduous or child teeth, mark the underlying phases of human dentition. Their rise is a visual demonstration of the development and improvement of a kid, framing a sequential record of a daily existence in steady motion. However, their possible shedding leads to a strong imagery — an imagery that addresses the certainty of progress, the progression of time, and the delicate weakness epitomized in the early years.

In thinking about the imagery of milk teeth, one is attracted to their unblemished whiteness and small size. It is in these characteristics that the illustration of immaculateness and weakness tracks down its underlying foundations. Milk teeth, immaculate by the intricacies of the world, address the clean guiltlessness of experience growing up. Their size, as opposed to the bigger and more strong super durable teeth that will follow, addresses the delicacy of this phase of life. The imagery lies in the juxtaposition between the fragile idea of milk teeth and the strong difficulties that lie ahead.

Socially, the shedding of milk teeth has been joined by ceremonies and customs that praise a kid's progress into another period of life. The tooth pixie, an eccentric figure in Western old stories, is one such sign of this social affirmation. In this practice, kids place their lost milk teeth under their pads around evening time, and the tooth pixie, a legendary substance, trades them for a little prize. This lively custom not just denotes the actual progress from child teeth to super durable teeth yet additionally turns into an enchanting affirmation of the youngster's development.

In addition, the imagery of milk teeth stretches out past individual encounters and into the aggregate stories woven into social orders. In writing, craftsmanship, and film, milk teeth are frequently utilized as images of immaculateness, weakness, and the transient idea of experience growing up. They become story gadgets that bring out a feeling of wistfulness, provoking reflection on the transient magnificence of youth and the inflexible walk of time.

The account unfurls further as we dig into the social and cultural assumptions interweaved with the imagery of milk teeth. Across different societies, the deficiency of the principal milk tooth is many times seen as a transitional experience — an emblematic marker that flags a kid's status for more noteworthy obligations and difficulties. The imagery reaches out past the singular experience to turn into a common story, an aggregate affirmation of the certainty of development and change.

The imagery of milk teeth likewise incorporates an organic transformation. These deciduous teeth act as brief placeholders for the long-lasting dentition that will arise later in an individual's life. The shedding of milk teeth, in this manner, turns into a characteristic and successive interaction, reflecting the repetitive idea of presence. In this organic mood, there is a beautiful reverberation — the old clearing a path for the new, the transient respecting the super durable.

Language and correspondence, as well, assume a part in the imagery of milk teeth. The rise of a youngster's most memorable teeth, the milk teeth, frequently corresponds with the improvement of language abilities. The jabbering of babies develops into the explanation of first words, denoting a critical stage in the kid's excursion toward self-articulation. The imagery lies in the possibility that the immaculateness of early correspondence, immaculate by the intricacies of grown-up talk, tracks down its lined up in the perfect whiteness of milk teeth.

Besides, the imagery of milk teeth is complicatedly associated with the ideas of trust and reliance. In the early long stretches of life as a youngster, a kid's confidence in their guardians is steady. The dependence on guardians or watchmen for food, care, and direction is reflected in the dependence on milk teeth for the underlying phases of biting and sustenance. The imagery lies in this harmonious relationship — a relationship established in trust, weakness, and the intrinsic interconnectedness of parental figure and youngster.

As the story advances, it mulls over the representative associations between milk teeth and character. The development of extremely durable teeth means actual development as well as a more profound investigation of selfhood. The imagery lies in the possibility that, as the kid sheds the last remnants of youth, they step into a more nuanced comprehension of their personality. The milk teeth become markers of a past time, nostalgic tokens of the straightforwardness and immaculateness that portray the early years.

In looking at the imagery of milk teeth, the story returns to the social and cultural aspects, perceiving that these images develop across time and various networks. The smoothness of imagery is reflected in the assorted ways societies decipher and praise the shedding of milk teeth. The account turns into an investigation of the rich woven artwork of convictions and works on, highlighting the widespread topics of development, change, and the versatility of the human soul.

The profound scene encompassing the idea of the tooth pixie is likewise investigated inside this emblematic account. Past its lively and capricious nature, the tooth pixie custom turns into a social articulation of parental consideration and support. The little prize left by the tooth pixie fills in as a substantial affirmation of the kid's mental fortitude in confronting the vulnerabilities of progress.

A ceremonial scaffolds the nonexistent with the genuine, making a space for youngsters to explore the profound intricacies of growing up.

Besides, the imagery of milk teeth welcomes reflection on the job of guardians in directing youngsters through these changes. Parental figures become stewards of this representative excursion, offering both the help expected to explore change and the space for the youngster to attest their arising character. The fragile dance between clutching the leftovers of experience growing up and empowering the kid to step into the unknown region of puberty turns into a significant affirmation of the extraordinary power innate in the imagery of milk teeth.

The story nimbly closes by welcoming perusers to consider the getting through imagery of milk teeth — an imagery that rises above social and transient limits. It is an investigation of the all inclusive subjects woven into the texture of this illustration — topics of honesty, flexibility, misfortune, and the ceaseless pattern of development and change.

The milk teeth, in their temporary presence, become gatekeepers of an immortal story — one that unfurls in the hearts of kids, parental figures, and social orders the same. As the imagery of milk teeth continues, it remains as a demonstration of the getting through force of illustration, molding how we might interpret the fragile dance among honesty and experience.

Chapter 3

Lost and Found

Itself through the synchronicity of lost and tracked down encounters.

In the woven artwork of "Lost and Found," the account explores the territory of existential addressing. It considers the essential requests that emerge while confronting misfortunes — inquiries concerning importance, reason, and the idea of presence. The demonstration of finding turns into a significant reaction to these requests, a disclosure that, amidst life's vulnerabilities, there are epiphanies and importance ready to be revealed.

The investigation of "Lost and Found" digs into the profound range that goes with these encounters. Misfortune, with its powerful hurt, is an all inclusive human inclination. It resounds in the quiet halls of sadness, resonates in the reverberations of awfulness, and waits in the spaces left empty by what used to be. The story turns into an investigation of the bunch feelings that go with misfortune — misery, distress, yearning, and the sensitive hit the dance floor with acknowledgment. It perceives that the demonstration of finding, in its embodiment, is frequently joined by feelings of bliss, alleviation, and the delicate warmth of rediscovery.

As the story unfurls, it thinks about the edges of weakness and fortitude that portray the "Lost and Found" venture. The weakness inborn in recognizing a misfortune, whether unmistakable or elusive, requires a gutsy showdown with the void it abandons. The demonstration of finding, then, at that point, turns into a demonstration of strength — a fearless move toward mending, reconstructing, and it was lost to recover what. It is inside this exchange of weakness and mental fortitude that the story tracks down the dauntless soul of the human experience.

The topic of "Lost and Found" broadens its ringlets into the domain of otherworldliness and contemplation. It turns into an excursion of the spirit — a mission for self-revelation, greatness, and a more profound comprehension of the interconnectedness, everything being equal. The story turns into an investigation of the manners by which profound practices, whether established in custom or individual way of thinking, give comfort, direction, and a compass for exploring the intricacies of misfortune and rediscovery.

With regards to vocation and life ways, the account ponders the luck and purposefulness that shape proficient and individual directions. Professions might go off in strange directions, aspirations might be recalibrated, and the quest for enthusiasm might prompt unanticipated disclosures. The story turns into a contemplation on the manners by which people explore the maze of expert and individual decisions, in some cases coincidentally finding unforeseen open doors that rethink the course of their lives.

The investigation of "Lost and Found" inside the setting of social accounts recognizes the force of aggregate narrating. Social fantasies, fables, and legends frequently rotate around subjects of misfortune and rediscovery, becoming prototype stories that reverberate across ages. The story turns into an acknowledgment of the persevering through effect of these accounts, filling in as guideposts for people and networks exploring their own "Lost and Found" ventures.

Also, the story stops to consider the job of innovation and advancement in the "Lost and Found" account. During a time where computerized impressions and virtual associations shape our lives, the idea of misfortune and disclosure takes on new aspects. The story turns into an investigation of the manners by which innovation works with both the detachment and reconnection of lives, making virtual scenes where lost associations can be rediscovered and new ones fashioned.

The topic of "Lost and Found" additionally envelops the natural and environmental components of the human experience. The deficiency of biodiversity, the debasement of environments, and the rediscovery of feasible practices become vital pieces of the story. The investigation turns into a consideration of humankind's interconnectedness with the normal world and the obligation to rediscover agreeable approaches to coinciding with the planet.

Inside the domain of instruction, the story considers the significant effect of learning and information as vehicles for individual and aggregate revelation. The deficiency of obliviousness and the securing of astuteness become groundbreaking minutes in the instructive excursion. The story turns into a festival of the educators, tutors, and instructive encounters that guide people through the maze of getting the hang of, assisting them with tracking down information as well as a more profound comprehension of themselves and the world.

With regards to cultural and political scenes, the account dives into the intricacies of aggregate misfortunes and revelations. Cultural disturbances, political unrests, and social renaissances become sections in the bigger story of mankind. The account turns into an investigation of the manners by which social orders wrestle with the misfortunes of blamelessness, equity, and opportunity, while additionally finding flexibility, solidarity, and the potential for extraordinary change.

As the story winds through these different components of "Lost and Found," it highlights the recurrent and interconnected nature of these encounters. Misfortunes are not disconnected occasions but rather basic parts of the human excursion, interlacing with snapshots of revelation, development, and recharging. The story turns into a thought of the complicated dance between the shadows of what is lost and the enlightening light of what is found.

The topic of "Lost and Found" unfurls as a diverse investigation of the human experience. It crosses the scenes of individual connections, self-revelation, strength, otherworldliness, vocation ways, social stories, mechanical impacts, ecological cognizance, schooling, and cultural elements. Inside each aspect, the story unwinds the layers of significance, welcoming consideration on the significant and ground-breaking nature of the "Lost and Found" venture. It turns into a demonstration of the versatility of the human soul, the insight acquired through misfortunes, and the interminable limit with respect to rediscovery that characterizes the many-sided embroidery of our lives.

In the broad material of human life, the theme of "Lost and Found" endures as a powerful story, winding around its strings through the rich embroidery of our lives. The investigation of this subject digs further into its unpredictable layers, unwinding the significant intricacies intrinsic in the exchange of misfortune and rediscovery.

At its pith, "Lost and Found" exemplifies the repetitive beat of life — a ceaseless dance between snapshots of partition and gathering, nonattendance and presence, fracture and completeness. It coaxes people to set out on a thoughtful excursion, thinking about the subtleties of losing and, thusly, finding. This investigation turns into a philosophical mission, a reflection on the idea of temporariness, strength, and the groundbreaking power implanted inside the texture of human experience.

The story unfurls against the setting of unmistakable misfortunes that manifest in the actual domain. These misfortunes might appear as treasured belongings, unmistakable associations, or even the moving scenes of our outer climate. The removal of a nostalgic curio, the disintegration of a once-dear kinship, or the reshaping of recognizable environmental elements — all become parts in the adventure of "Lost and Found." Inside these unmistakable misfortunes, the story finds the intrinsic temporariness of material presence, welcoming thought on the transient idea of assets and the getting through reverberations they leave in the halls of memory.

At the same time, the investigation stretches out into the domain of elusive misfortunes, where feelings, connections, and features of personality go through change. Sadness, with its significant reverberation, turns into a strong buddy in this investigation. The story turns into a reflection on the close to home scenes navigated during seasons of misfortune — the profound wells of distress, the many-sided hit the dance floor with yearning, and the slow rise of acknowledgment. It is inside the hug of these feelings that people explore the maze of "Lost and Found," manufacturing a cozy association with the recurring pattern of the human heart.

As the story wanders through the scene of individual connections, it considers the transient idea of associations — a fragile dance between brief experiences and getting through bonds. Companionships might disappear, close connections might break down, and familial ties might go through changes. The account turns into an affirmation of the consistently changing elements inside human connections, perceiving that during the time spent losing, there is in many cases an implicit greeting for freshly discovered associations with flourish.

The investigation expands its ringlets into the domains of self-disclosure and self-improvement. The excursion of ending up in the midst of the maze of life turns into a point of convergence. The story turns into a thoughtful mission, exploring the forms of personality, reason, and the advancing identity. Misfortunes, whether as broken deceptions or the shedding of obsolete accounts, become impetuses for rediscovery — an encouragement to investigate the immense scenes of inside territory and embrace the unending system of becoming.

The subject of "Lost and Found" secures a transient aspect as the story ponders the progression of time. The ticking of the clock turns into a determined buddy, forming the stories of our lives with its sequential beats. In this worldly dance, misfortunes collect as markers of minutes gone by, while disclosures unfurl as the commitments of minutes on the way. The story turns into a reflection on the certainty of progress, the recurrent idea of presence, and the immortal repeats that resonate across the continuum of time.

Inside the cultural setting, the investigation of "Lost and Found" recognizes the aggregate idea of these encounters. Cultural movements, social changes, and verifiable retributions become essential strings in the bigger story. The story turns into a thought of how social orders wrestle with the misfortunes of aggregate guiltlessness, equity, and social legacy, while at the same time finding strength, solidarity, and the potential for aggregate reestablishment.

Besides, the story stops to think about the job of innovation and advancement in molding the scene of "Lost and Found." In a period where computerized impressions and virtual associations entwine with the texture of our lives, the idea of misfortune and revelation takes on new aspects. The story turns into an investigation of the manners by which innovation works with both disengagement and reconnection, making virtual scenes where lost associations can be rediscovered, and new ones fashioned.

In the domain of schooling, the account considers the groundbreaking force of learning and information as vehicles for individual and aggregate revelation. The deficiency of obliviousness and the obtaining of shrewdness become extraordinary achievements in the instructive excursion. The story turns into a festival of the instructors, coaches, and instructive encounters that guide people through the maze of getting the hang of, assisting them with tracking down information as well as a more profound comprehension of themselves and the world.

The topic of "Lost and Found" unfurls inside the setting of profound and philosophical request. It turns into an excursion of the spirit — a mission for greatness, meaning, and a more profound comprehension of the interconnectedness, everything being equal. The story turns into an investigation of the manners by which otherworldly practices, whether established in custom or individual way of thinking, give comfort, direction, and a compass for exploring the intricacies of misfortune and rediscovery.

The account dives into the close to home scenes encompassing the "Lost and Found" story, perceiving that the demonstration of finding is frequently joined by feelings of happiness, alleviation, and the delicate warmth of rediscovery. These profound shades become fundamental to the story, painting a nuanced picture of the human involvement with all its intricacy.

In looking at the convergences of possibility and deliberateness inside the topic of "Lost and Found," the account considers the job of luck in molding our directions. Fortunate experiences, unforeseen reunions, and the accidental disclosure of direction or energy become central places of investigation. It is inside these snapshots of chance that the story tracks down a component of wizardry — an update that in the midst of the mayhem of life, there exists a secretive request that periodically uncovers itself.

The investigation of "Lost and Found" broadens its ringlets into the natural and biological components of the human experience. The deficiency of biodiversity, the corruption of environments, and the rediscovery of maintainable practices become vital pieces of the story. The investigation turns into an examination of humankind's interconnectedness with the regular world and the obligation to rediscover agreeable approaches to coinciding with the planet.

The story ponders the significant effect of imaginative articulation as a focal point through which to investigate the subject of "Lost and Found." Craftsmanship, whether visual, melodic, or scholarly, turns into a vessel for the enunciation of the human experience, offering nuanced reflections on misfortune, rediscovery, and the groundbreaking influence of innovative articulation.

Inside the setting of cultural and political scenes, the account considers the intricacies of aggregate misfortunes and disclosures. Cultural disturbances, political upsets, and social renaissances become parts in the bigger account of humankind. The account turns into an investigation of the manners by which social orders wrestle with the misfortunes of guiltlessness, equity, and opportunity, while additionally finding versatility, solidarity, and the potential for extraordinary change.

As the account winds through these different elements of "Lost and Found," it highlights the recurrent and interconnected nature of these encounters. Misfortunes are not secluded occasions but rather necessary parts of the human excursion, interlacing with snapshots of revelation, development, and recharging. The story turns into a thought of the mind boggling dance between the shadows of what is lost and the enlightening light of what is found.

The topic of "Lost and Found" unfurls as a complex investigation of the human experience. It crosses the scenes of individual connections, self-disclosure, strength, otherworldliness, vocation ways, social accounts, mechanical impacts, natural cognizance, schooling, and cultural elements. Inside each aspect, the story disentangles the layers of significance, welcoming thought on the significant and groundbreaking nature of the "Lost and Found" venture. It turns into a demonstration of the versatility of the human soul, the insight acquired through misfortunes, and the never-ending limit with respect to rediscovery that characterizes the complex embroidery of our lives.

3.1. Adventures of the Tooth Fairy

In the captivating domain of young life, where creative mind exceeds all rational limitations and wonderment is an everyday buddy, the Experiences of the Tooth Pixie unfurl as an enchanted embroidery woven with caprice, euphoria, and the sensitive hint of pixie dust.

The Tooth Pixie, a cherished legendary figure in the old stories of many societies, becomes the overwhelming focus in this story, leaving on fantastical excursions to gather the small fortunes abandoned by kids as they bid goodbye to their milk teeth. The Experiences of the Tooth Pixie become a festival of the widespread soul changing experience — the deficiency of child teeth — and the captivating practices that go with this excursion.

The story starts with the appearance of the Tooth Pixie just before a youngster's originally lost tooth. In the tranquil quiet of night, as the world sleeps, the Tooth Pixie rises up out of the supernatural domain where dreams and reality unite. Embellished in a sparkling outfit that mirrors the tints of twilight, her wings shimmering with stardust, the Tooth Pixie conveys a little handbag and a wand that sparkles with the commitment of charm. Her process initiates as she vacillates down to the homes of dozing youngsters, directed by the delicate sparkle of night.

The Undertakings of the Tooth Pixie reach out past simple assortment, rising above into an eccentric investigation of the extraordinary conditions encompassing each lost tooth. Whether settled under a pad, put in an extraordinary compartment, or even secret in a painstakingly created tooth pixie house, every tooth conveys its own story. The Tooth Pixie turns into a quiet narrator, unraveling the messages left by youngsters and, thusly, abandoning badge of enchantment — a sprinkle of pixie dust, a manually written note, or maybe a little knickknack that mirrors the kid's fantasies.

As the story unfurls, the Tooth Pixie experiences a heap of creative situations. In one captivating experience, she explores a tooth charmed with the wish of a future space traveler, abandoning a heavenly body of stars under the pad. In one more unusual story, a tooth pervaded with the longing to be an artist prompts the Tooth Pixie to leave a little expressive dance shoe in its place. The Experiences of the Tooth Pixie become a kaleidoscope of innovativeness, where each lost tooth turns into a material for dreams to take off.

The account stops to investigate the assorted social practices that go with the Tooth Pixie's visits. In certain societies, youngsters place their lost teeth in an exceptionally created tooth pocket, while in others, the tooth is covered underneath a tree with the expectation that another tooth will develop further as the roots. These social subtleties add layers to the Undertakings of the Tooth Pixie, outlining the embroidery of worldwide old stories woven around the common experience of losing child teeth.

As the Tooth Pixie proceeds with her nighttime odyssey, she experiences the delicate feelings that go with the passing of a tooth. The story turns into a sympathetic investigation of the blend of fervor and wistfulness that fills a youngster's heart as they head out in different directions from a piece of their guiltlessness. The Tooth Pixie, with her ethereal presence, turns into a consoling friend, a watchman of the fleeting idea of young life, and a harbinger of the development that goes with the shedding of milk teeth.

The Undertakings of the Tooth Pixie likewise dig into the fables and folklore that encompass this charming person. In different societies, the Tooth Pixie isn't simply a singular substance however part of a bigger cast of mysterious creatures. In certain customs, a tooth mouse assumes the job of gatherer, while in others, the tooth is thrown onto the rooftop with the expectation that a kindhearted soul will trade it for a coin. These legendary partners improve the enchanted emanation of the Tooth Pixie's experiences, making a feeling of interconnectedness in the worldwide festival of this youth achievement.

In addition, the account investigates the agelessness of the Tooth Pixie's presence, rising above ages and making a permanent imprint on the aggregate memory of young life. Guardians who once positioned their lost teeth under cushions presently proceed with the custom with their own kids, passing down the tradition of the Tooth Pixie's visits. The Undertakings of the Tooth Pixie become a continuum of charm, associating the past, present, and future in an embroidery of shared happiness and marvel.

In the captivating scene of the Tooth Pixie's experiences, the account presents eccentric mates that join her on her daily journeys. Chipper pixies, naughty sprites, and savvy forest animals become partners in the amazing undertaking of gathering lost teeth. Together, they arrange snapshots of wizardry that unfurl in the quiet spaces of dozing homes, making an environment of charm that waits long after the Tooth Pixie's flight.

The story likewise welcomes perusers to investigate the connection between the Tooth Pixie and the divine domains. The Tooth Pixie, it is uncovered, has a heavenly partner — an ethereal element that manages the night sky and organizes the vast dance of lost teeth. The Undertakings of the Tooth Pixie take on an interstellar aspect as she teams up with heavenly allies to pervade each lost tooth with the radiance of far off stars. This divine association adds a heavenly layer to the charm, raising the Tooth Pixie's experiences to an enormous expressive dance of miracle.

As the Tooth Pixie vacillates from one home to another, the story unfurls as a festival of the different dreams and goals held onto by youngsters. Each lost tooth turns into a vessel for these goals, a little encouraging sign and creative mind. The Tooth Pixie, in her job as a caretaker of dreams, turns into a gatekeeper of the boundless potential that dwells inside the hearts of kids, sustaining their faith in the enchanted that winds through the texture of life as a youngster.

In investigating the Undertakings of the Tooth Pixie, the account embraces the idea of correspondence and appreciation. Youngsters, in their honesty, offer thanks to the Tooth Pixie through transcribed notes, drawings, and, surprisingly, little gifts left in kind.

The Tooth Pixie, contacted by these signals, responds with articulations of bliss — a twist of pixie dust, a genuine reaction in sensitive content, or maybe an additional sprinkle of sorcery to enlighten the youngster's fantasies. The story turns into a demonstration of the force of appreciation in making a proportional dance of charm.

The account additionally digs into the fleeting idea of the Tooth Pixie's undertakings, unfurling on single evenings as well as throughout the span of innumerable nights. The progression of time turns into a piercing propensity, denoting the change from the principal lost tooth to the last. The Experiences of the Tooth Pixie become a narrative of life as a youngster's momentary minutes, an update that the wizardry of blamelessness is a valuable gift that is both treasured and surrendered as the years unfurl.

Inside the setting of the Tooth Pixie's undertakings, the story examines the pith of young life itself — when faith in the phenomenal isn't just supported yet celebrated. The Tooth Pixie, with her enchanted undertakings, turns into a caretaker of this conviction, cultivating a climate where youngsters can embrace the fantastical and mesh their fantasies into the texture of the real world. The account turns into a tribute to the getting through soul of young life, where the standard is changed into the phenomenal from the perspective of miracle and creative mind.

As the story wanders through the unconventional scenes of the Tooth Pixie's experiences, it welcomes perusers to think about the more extensive meaning of these appreciated practices. The demonstration of gathering lost teeth, joined by the trading of tokens and the sprinkling of pixie dust, turns into a custom that rises above the material domain. It turns into a festival of development, strength, and the immortal sorcery woven into the embroidery of human experience.

In a sincere investigation of the Undertakings of the Tooth Pixie, the story highlights the significance of protecting these customs as a fundamental piece of experience growing up's heritage. The Tooth Pixie's charming ventures, with their mix of wizardry and delicacy, add to the rich social woven artwork that characterizes the common encounters of ages. The story turns into a call to esteem these snapshots of guiltlessness, to shield the confidence in the uncommon, and to pass down the tradition of marvel starting with one age then onto the next.

The Undertakings of the Tooth Pixie likewise act as a similitude for the more extensive excursion of growing up — an odyssey set apart by the shedding of honesty, the hug of progress, and the revelation of new features of self. The Tooth Pixie turns into a representative aide, exploring youngsters through the changes innate in the entry from youth to immaturity. The story turns into a delicate update that, similarly as the Tooth Pixie gathers the badge of experience growing up, life itself unfurls as an assortment of minutes, each saturated with its own wizardry and importance.

In a powerful investigation of the Undertakings of the Tooth Pixie, that's what the story recognizes, at last, the opportunity arrives when the visits stop, and the enchanted takes on an alternate structure. The deficiency of child teeth marks the finish of a part as well as the start of another one — an unfurling venture into the domains of youthfulness and adulthood. The story turns into a self-contradicting reflection on the certainty of progress, the flexibility of the human soul, and the getting through tradition of experience growing up's charm.

In the charming domain of life as a youngster, where the cloak among the real world and creative mind is at its most slender, the Experiences of the Tooth Pixie keep on unfurling with a persevering through wizardry that rises above time. As the moon gives occasion to feel qualms about its shimmering gleam sleeping families, the Tooth Pixie, with gossamer wings and a heart overflowing with charm, sets out on daily stays to gather the little fortunes abandoned by kids saying farewell to their child teeth. In this ethereal dance among dreams and reality, the Undertakings of the Tooth Pixie become an ensemble of happiness, wonder, and the immortal festival of a widespread soul changing experience — the deficiency of milk teeth.

The account, with its multicolored focal point, looks into the nighttime adventures of the Tooth Pixie, whose appearance is proclaimed by the delicate quiet of dusk. Clad in an outfit woven from the strings of moonbeams and embellished with a headdress that sparkles like far off stars, she slides upon the homes of sleeping youngsters, directed by the iridescence of her wand. In the quietude of these minutes, the wizardry of the Tooth Pixie spreads out, and the experiences start.

Each lost tooth, painstakingly settled underneath a cushion or supported in a unique compartment, turns into an entry to a universe of charm. The Tooth Pixie, with her keen look, unravels the quiet wishes implanted in these little fortunes. A tooth imbued with the fantasy about turning into a wayfarer could summon a path of pixie impressions prompting a little money box, while a tooth seeking to be a painter could rouse the making of a small material embellished with ethereal strokes of variety. The Experiences of the Tooth Pixie in this manner become a material for imagination, where each lost tooth transformations into a vessel for dreams to take off.

As the story unfurls, it delicately explores the different social scenes that shape the practices encompassing the Tooth Pixie's visits. In certain edges of the world, youngsters get their lost teeth into uncommonly created tooth pockets, while in others, the teeth find their resting place underneath the earth with the desire for major areas of strength for encouraging, substitutions. These social subtleties add profundity to the Undertakings of the Tooth Pixie, showing the rich woven artwork of worldwide legends that merges upon the common experience of losing child teeth.

The eccentric stories likewise welcome perusers to investigate the profound reverberation that goes with the flight of a tooth. The story turns into a delicate investigation of the blending feelings — the fervor of an innocuous smile, the wistfulness for the momentary snapshots of life as a youngster, and the expectation of development typified in the rise of extremely durable teeth. The Tooth Pixie, with her ethereal presence, becomes a gatherer of actual tokens as well as a quiet observer to the nuanced feelings that wind through the texture of the human heart during this strong progress.

In navigating the Undertakings of the Tooth Pixie, the story gives recognition to the legends and folklore joined with this charming person. From tooth mice in certain societies to considerate spirits in others, the Tooth Pixie frequently has fanciful partners who share in the supernatural obligation of gathering lost teeth. These mythic associations enhance the charm of the Tooth Pixie's experiences, highlighting the general idea of this esteemed youth custom.

Additionally, the story stretches out a challenge to investigate the divine components of the Tooth Pixie's domain. In this ethereal artful dance, the Tooth Pixie teams up with heavenly partners — an ethereal substance administering the night sky — to pervade each lost tooth with the flicker of far off stars. The Experiences of the Tooth Pixie take on an interstellar quality, where the moon turns into a reference point, directing the nighttime mission and imbuing every tooth with the brilliance of vast marvels.

The story acquaints perusers with the capricious friends that join the Tooth Pixie on her nighttime journeys. Sporty pixies, wicked imps, and shrewd forest animals become partners in the excellent undertaking of gathering lost teeth. Together, they coordinate snapshots of sorcery that unfurl in the calm spaces of resting homes, making a climate of charm that waits long after the Tooth Pixie's takeoff.

These unusual colleagues, with their particular characters, add to the rich woven artwork of the Experiences of the Tooth Pixie.

The investigation of the Tooth Pixie's experiences likewise unfurls as a festival of the different dreams and goals held onto by kids. Each lost tooth turns into a vessel for these yearnings, a little encouraging sign and creative mind. The Tooth Pixie, in her job as a caretaker of dreams, turns into a gatekeeper of the boundless potential that lives inside the hearts of youngsters, supporting their faith in the enchanted that winds through the texture of experience growing up.

As the account dives into the fleeting idea of the Tooth Pixie's experiences, it unfurls not just on single evenings but rather over innumerable nights. The progression of time turns into an impactful propensity, denoting the change from the main lost tooth to the last. The Experiences of the Tooth Pixie become a narrative of young life's passing minutes, an update that the enchantment of honesty is a valuable gift that is both esteemed and surrendered as the years unfurl.

Inside the setting of the Tooth Pixie's undertakings, the story considers the embodiment of experience growing up — when faith in the exceptional isn't just empowered yet celebrated. The Tooth Pixie, with her supernatural undertakings, turns into an overseer of this conviction, encouraging a climate where youngsters can embrace the fantastical and mesh their fantasies into the texture of the real world. The story turns into a tribute to the getting through soul of experience growing up, where the normal is changed into the phenomenal from the perspective of marvel and creative mind.

In a sincere investigation of the Undertakings of the Tooth Pixie, the story highlights the significance of safeguarding these customs as a basic piece of life as a youngster's heritage. The Tooth Pixie's captivating ventures, with their mix of sorcery and delicacy, add to the rich social embroidery that characterizes the common encounters of ages. The story turns into a call to love these snapshots of honesty, to protect the faith in the remarkable, and to pass down the tradition of marvel starting with one age then onto the next.

The Undertakings of the Tooth Pixie likewise act as a representation for the more extensive excursion of growing up — an odyssey set apart by the shedding of guiltlessness, the hug of progress, and the revelation of new features of self. The Tooth Pixie turns into an emblematic aide, exploring youngsters through the changes innate in the entry from youth to immaturity. The story turns into a delicate update that, similarly as the Tooth Pixie gathers the badge of experience growing up, life itself unfurls as an assortment of minutes, each pervaded with its own wizardry and importance.

In a powerful investigation of the Undertakings of the Tooth Pixie, that's what the story recognizes, in the long run, the opportunity arrives when the visits stop, and the enchanted takes on an alternate structure. The deficiency of child teeth marks the finish of a section as well as the start of another one — an unfurling venture into the domains of pre-adulthood and adulthood. The story turns into a self-contradicting reflection on the certainty of progress, the strength of the human soul, and the persevering through tradition of young life's charm.

The Undertakings of the Tooth Pixie unfurl as an immortal and captivating excursion — a festival of the widespread experience of losing child teeth and the mysterious practices that go with this valued achievement. Through eccentric stories, social subtleties, and heavenly associations, the story winds around an embroidery of marvel, welcoming perusers to embrace the wizardry of blamelessness and the getting through soul of experience growing up.

The Tooth Pixie, with her ethereal presence, turns into a treasured watchman of dreams, an overseer of appreciation, and a signal of charm in the hearts of kids. The Experiences of the Tooth Pixie, in their fantastical quality, become a demonstration of the groundbreaking force of conviction, the delight of correspondence, and the persevering through wizardry that dwells inside the immortal hallways of young life's creative mind.

3.2. Tradition and folklore surrounding lost teeth

In the rich embroidery of human culture and legends, the practice encompassing lost teeth arises as a general and charming string that winds through the texture of different social orders. The demonstration of losing child teeth, a soul changing experience denoting the progress from youth to puberty, is joined by a heap of customs and convictions that differ across societies yet share a consistent idea of miracle and imagery.

The Captivated Progress:

In many societies, the passing of a youngster's most memorable tooth is a groundbreaking event, meaning a vital stage in their development and improvement. The progress from deciduous to extremely durable teeth is frequently celebrated with ceremonies that mirror the social qualities and convictions of a local area. This charming excursion is many times seen as a scaffold between the guiltlessness of young life and the arising consciousness of adulthood.

The Tooth Pixie's Worldwide Odyssey:

One of the most dearest customs encompassing lost teeth is the eccentric story of the Tooth Pixie. While the subtleties might contrast across societies, the quintessence continues as before — an ethereal being who gathers kids' lost teeth, abandoning badge of enchantment or little rewards. In Western societies, the Tooth Pixie is a jaunty animal who trades lost teeth for coins or little gifts, while in different regions of the planet, the Tooth Pixie might appear as a mouse, a bird, or even a considerate soul.

Social Subtleties in Tooth Assortment:

The demonstration of gathering lost teeth frequently stretches out past the Tooth Pixie account, uncovering different social subtleties. In certain societies, kids place their lost teeth in extraordinarily made compartments or pockets, while others cover the teeth to guarantee solid, sound substitutions. The techniques for tooth removal are weighed down with imagery, reflecting social convictions about the repetitive idea of life and the interconnectedness of the human experience.

Fanciful Partners:

Interesting fanciful sidekicks frequently go with the practice of lost teeth. From tooth mice to spirits and mystical animals, these creatures assume a part in gathering and defending the disposed of teeth. In Hispanic societies, for instance, the Ratón de los Dientes (Tooth Mouse) assumes on the liability of gathering teeth, accentuating the association among old stories and the ordinary encounters of growing up.

Divine Associations:

The divine domain isn't safe to the impact of lost teeth customs. A few societies accept that the place of the moon or stars during the tooth misfortune impacts the qualities of the arising long-lasting teeth. The heavenly dance becomes interwoven with the natural custom, adding a component of astronomical persona to the experience.

Transitional experiences and Functions:

The deficiency of child teeth frequently denotes a more extensive transitional experience, with services and ceremonies that fluctuate generally across societies. In Japan, the Shichi-Go-San celebration praises the development of kids at the ages of three, five, and seven, including the visit to a holy place to petition God for a youngster's solid teeth. These functions highlight the social importance joined to the physical and emblematic progress from essential to super durable dentition.

Imagery and Odd notions:

Lost teeth are loaded down with imagery and, in certain societies, odd notions. The shape, size, and area of the lost tooth might be accepted to predict parts of the youngster's future. In Russia, for instance, it is viewed as amazing good fortune to toss a lost tooth over the edge of the youngster's home, while in different societies, covering the tooth is remembered to bring thriving.

Familial Association:

In specific societies, lost teeth are seen as private achievements as well as associations with familial spirits. The demonstration of disposing of a tooth turns into a custom that rises above individual experience, recognizing the recurrent idea of life and the intergenerational connection between past, present, and future.

Instructive Drives:

The custom of lost teeth isn't bound to the domain of old stories; it has likewise tracked down its direction into instructive drives. A few schools and instructive projects consolidate examples or exercises connected with dental wellbeing, utilizing the experience of losing teeth as a workable second to impart positive oral cleanliness propensities in kids.

Advancement of Customs:

As social orders advance, so do the customs encompassing lost teeth. The globalization of societies has prompted a sharing of customs, with the Tooth Pixie story rising above geological limits. In any case, even as customs become more general, the nearby subtleties and remarkable social articulations keep on forming the manner in which networks commend this capricious and charming part of experience growing up.

The Job of Present day Media:

In contemporary times, present day media, including writing, movies, and TV, plays had an impact in molding the story around lost teeth. Characters like the Tooth Pixie have become notorious figures in kids' accounts, further implanting the custom in the social cognizance. These depictions frequently mix old legends with contemporary narrating, making a scaffold between the old and the new.

Safeguarding of Social Legacy:

While globalization has prompted the sharing of customs, there is a developing familiarity with the significance of safeguarding social legacy. Endeavors to report and renew native practices connected with lost teeth guarantee that the lavishness and variety of these customs are passed down to people in the future, keeping an association with social roots.

In diving further into the complex embroidery of custom and old stories encompassing lost teeth, it becomes apparent that this apparently basic demonstration of shedding deciduous teeth conveys significant social importance, winding around together strings of folklore, imagery, and public rituals. The variety of practices across various societies and districts not just features the comprehensiveness of the human experience yet additionally highlights the remarkable manners by which social orders have looked to get a handle on this normal progress from youth to pre-adulthood.

Legendary Strings:

Inside the rich story of lost teeth, legendary strings are entwined, making an intricate embroidery that rises above the limits of time and topography. These fantasies frequently offer clarifications for the starting points of the custom and give a social setting to the importance credited to the demonstration of losing teeth. Whether it be the Tooth Pixie in Western societies, the Ratón de los Dientes in Hispanic practices, or other legendary creatures in different social orders, these stories add layers of charm and marvel to the experience of growing up.

Imagery Implanted in Ceremonies:

At the core of lost teeth customs lies imagery that goes past the actual demonstration itself. The customs related with tooth misfortune frequently convey profound analogies connected with development, development, and the repetitive idea of life. The stylized angles, whether through covering teeth, offering them to legendary animals, or performing explicit customs, become emblematic extensions between the guiltlessness of experience growing up and the obligations of adulthood. These customs act as common markers, supporting shared values and convictions inside a social setting.

Territorial Varieties in Tooth Assortment:

While the Tooth Pixie is a darling figure in Western societies, the techniques and characters engaged with tooth assortment differ broadly across districts. In a few Asian societies, the lost tooth is much of the time put on the top of the house or took care of to creatures, representing an association with nature. In Center Eastern societies, the practice includes tossing the lost tooth onto the rooftop, with the expectation that it will be supplanted by areas of strength for a, exemplifying the social longing for strength and versatility.

Social Subtleties in Tooth Removal:

The removal of lost teeth, whether through entombment, contributions to creatures, or imaginative showcases, reflects social subtleties that are well established in nearby convictions. In Japan, for example, the Shichi-Go-San celebration praises the development of youngsters as well as includes a visit to a holy place to petition God for their sound teeth. The demonstration of covering teeth might represent an association with the earth, underlining the equal connection among mankind and nature.

Odd notions and Forecasts:

Past the prompt demonstration of tooth misfortune, strange notions and forecasts related with the shape, size, or area of the lost tooth add a fascinating layer to the old stories. In certain societies, the conviction that a tooth tossed into the sun will bring best of luck penetrates nearby traditions. The state of the lost tooth might be viewed as a sign, giving bits of knowledge into the kid's future. These notions add a component of secret as well as feature the crossing point of old stories with a general public's convictions about fate and fortune.

Divine Impacts on Tooth Misfortune:

The association between divine bodies and the demonstration of losing teeth acquaints one more aspect with these practices. Social convictions that interface the places of the moon, stars, or planets to the timing and qualities of tooth misfortune add to a feeling of inestimable interconnectedness. The night sky, in many societies, turns into a divine setting to the natural ceremonies, making an extension between the earthbound and the heavenly domains.

Rising above Ages through Schooling:

As customs encompassing lost teeth develop, schooling turns into a urgent channel through which these traditions are passed down starting with one age then onto the next. Schools and instructive projects that consolidate illustrations on dental wellbeing, social customs, and the imagery implanted in lost teeth guarantee that these practices are saved as well as figured out inside the more extensive setting of a general public's legacy. This instructive drive turns into a scaffold between the past and the present, cultivating an appreciation for social variety.

Impact of Current Media:

In the contemporary time, present day media, including writing, films, and computerized stages, has turned into a strong force to be reckoned with in molding the stories encompassing lost teeth. Characters like the Tooth Pixie, portrayed in mainstream society, add to the propagation and worldwide spread of these customs. The crossing point of old legends with present day narrating makes a powerful collaboration that keeps these traditions alive in the aggregate creative mind of networks.

Protection of Native Practices:

Endeavors to report and protect native practices connected with lost teeth are critical for shielding social legacy. As globalization brings different practices into contact, there is a developing acknowledgment of the significance of saving interesting traditions that might be in danger of disappearing. Drives pointed toward recording oral accounts, reporting customs, and elevating social trade add to the strength of these practices.

Social Transformations and Globalization:

The flexibility of social practices encompassing lost teeth is obvious in their capacity to coincide with worldwide impacts. While specific angles might go through changes or reevaluations, the center substance of these traditions continues. Globalization, instead of eradicating social qualifications, has worked with a cross-fertilization of thoughts, making a mosaic where different customs add to an aggregate human story.

Shared Enchantment of Life as a youngster:

At its center, the custom and old stories encompassing lost teeth inspire a feeling of shared wizardry that rises above social, semantic, and topographical limits. No matter what the particular ceremonies or legendary figures included, the demonstration of losing teeth is a generally human encounter, a soul changing experience that ties people to a more extensive aggregate story. In embracing the charm of lost teeth, social orders praise the general excursion from youth to pre-adulthood, joining different societies through a common acknowledgment of the miracles innate in growing up.

As the investigation of custom and fables encompassing lost teeth unfurls, it becomes clear that these traditions are not static relics of the past but rather living articulations of social personality. From legendary creatures to heavenly impacts, from representative ceremonies to instructive drives, the customs encompassing lost teeth stay dynamic, adjusting to the advancing scenes of social orders.

This rich embroidered artwork of old stories keeps on being woven, string by string, by networks across the globe, adding to the immortal story of human experience. In loving and understanding these customs, we find not just the different manners by which social orders have explored the change from milk teeth to long-lasting dentition yet additionally the persevering through enchantment that joins us in the common excursion of growing up.

3.3. The mysterious exchange: tooth for a treasure

In the tranquil domains of life as a youngster, an immortal and charming practice unfurls — a trade covered in secret, where the vaporous idea of youth joins with the appeal of fortunes. This magical practice, known as "The Puzzling Trade: Tooth for a Fortune," rises above social limits and ranges ages, providing reason to feel ambiguous about its spell the aggregate creative mind of youngsters and grown-ups the same.

At the core of this mysterious trade lies the unassuming milk tooth, a little remnant of youth shed in the excursion toward development. The demonstration of losing a tooth, a widespread soul changing experience, turns into an entrance to an existence where the customary changes into the exceptional. As the main tooth slackens its grasp, a youngster turns into an accidental member in a custom that has reverberated through the hallways of time, winding around its enchantment in the stories of endless societies.

In investigating "The Secretive Trade," one is brought into the unusual dance between the substantial and the elusive, the seen and the concealed. The expectation that goes with the squirming of a tooth turns into a preface to a covert meeting — a trade coordinated by powers concealed, yet profoundly felt in the hearts of the people who participate in this otherworldly practice.

The story of "The Strange Trade" frequently presents a kind figure, a harbinger of charm who rises above social differentiations. Whether known as the Tooth Pixie, a divine sprite, or a legendary being, this figure encapsulates the substance of the secretive trade. With wings that shine like evening glow and a wand that sparkles with the commitment of enchantment, the Tooth Pixie turns into the caretaker of this ethereal exchange.

As the kid puts the lost tooth underneath the cushion, a quieted hope pervades the evening. The Tooth Pixie, with an effortlessness that reflects the delicate stir of wind through leaves, plunges upon the resting residence. At this time, a domain of marvel and plausibility unfurls — a recess where the commonplace gives approach to the unprecedented, and the ordinary becomes moved by the hand of enchantment.

The actual trade conveys a feeling of correspondence, a sensitive harmony between the guiltlessness of the kid and the charm presented by the Tooth Pixie. As a trade-off for the contribution of a little ivory treasure, the kid stirs to find a symbolic abandoned — a glinting coin, a little knickknack, or maybe a transcribed note that communicates in the language of dreams. The trade turns into a dance of appreciation and marvel, an implicit affirmation of the transient idea of experience growing up and the immortal charm of sorcery.

Social subtleties mesh complicated designs into the texture of "The Baffling Trade," imbuing the practice with novel flavors intelligent of assorted social orders. In certain societies, the lost tooth finds another home in an uncommonly created tooth pocket, a vessel that supports the actual artifact as well as the deepest desires murmured in the calm of the evening. In others, the tooth might be ceremoniously covered, cultivating an association with the earth and the patterns of life.

However, past the unmistakable antiques and social ceremonies, the pith of "The Puzzling Trade" lies in ability to summon feelings reverberate all around. The kid, with eyes aglow in the first part of the day light, finds the fortune left by the Tooth Pixie — a transient second that embodies the delight, wonder, and short lived wizardry of youth. The trade turns into a standard, a memory scratched in the chronicles of growing up.

Diving into the verifiable foundations of this puzzling practice, one experiences antiquated convictions and folkloric customs that have formed the story of tooth misfortune. In Norse folklore, the goddess Frigg, in her generosity, gives gifts to kids who offer their lost teeth. Also, in different societies, teeth were accepted to have profound importance, filling in as vessels for the spirit or as defensive charms against pernicious powers.

The imagery implanted in "The Strange Trade" stretches out past the actual demonstration, digging into the allegorical scene of young life's transient minutes. The tooth, a transient remnant of youth, turns into a similitude for the progression of time — an update that the honesty of experience growing up is essentially as delicate and fleeting as the minuscule fortunes left underneath pads. In this powerful trade, the youngster gets a material token as well as looks into the elusive domains of memory and wistfulness.

The secretive dance of tooth for a fortune likewise welcomes consideration of the extraordinary influence inborn in conviction. The kid, with steady confidence in the concealed, takes part in this custom with a truthfulness that rises above suspicion. The Tooth Pixie, with her ethereal presence, turns into a sign of the confidence in enchantment — a conviction that cultivates a feeling of marvel and creative mind, characteristics that are frequently consigned to the domains of young life yet stay the wellspring of imagination and delight.

In the contemporary scene, "The Strange Trade" ends up weaved with advancement, developing close by the moving flows of culture and innovation. The coming of computerized correspondence considers a cutting edge contort, with youngsters making messages or messages to the Tooth Pixie, overcoming any barrier between old stories and the computerized age. However, in the midst of the cutting edge features, the center pith of the trade stays unaltered — the encapsulation of the enchanted and the fantastical in the standard embroidery of regular day to day existence.

The strange exchange of tooth for a fortune turns into a vessel for investigating the profound scene of growing up. The youngster, in saying goodbye to a tooth, makes a stride nearer to the domain of adulthood — a progress set apart by both energy and an unpretentious propensity of sentimentality. The Tooth Pixie, in her job as a quiet observer to this change, turns into a gatekeeper of the profound subtleties woven into the texture of the trade.

As "The Puzzling Trade" keeps on projecting its spell across ages, the account welcomes contemplation into the job of custom and custom in forming our impression of the world. The trade turns into a channel through which social qualities, convictions, and articulations of marvel are communicated, making an embroidery that connections past, present, and future. The kid who puts a tooth underneath the cushion turns into a torchbearer, conveying the fire of custom into the unfamiliar domains of their own youngsters' minds.

In the shadows of this strange trade, questions wait — questions that dive into the quintessence of conviction, the groundbreaking idea of custom, and the persevering through appeal of enchantment. What constrains a kid to confide in the concealed, to enthusiastically participate in a custom that challenges the objective and the observational?

Maybe it is the characteristic human yearning for charm, for minutes that rise above the ordinary and raise the soul. "The Puzzling Trade," in its straightforwardness, turns into a demonstration of the human ability to see as enchantment in the common, to support a conviction that rises above the limits of the known and wanders into the domains of endless chance.

The proceeded with investigation of "The Baffling Trade: Tooth for a Fortune" welcomes a more profound consideration of the nuanced layers that underlie this charming custom. As the story unfurls, the actual substance of the trade uncovers itself as a sensitive dance between the transient idea of young life and the getting through charm of fortunes both substantial and elusive.

At its center, the baffling trade fills in as an extension between the universes of creative mind and reality. The kid, in putting a little tooth underneath the cushion, participates in a peaceful demonstration of trust — a faith in the concealed, a confidence in the charm that winds through the texture of the normal. In this demonstration of trust, the kid ventures into a domain where the limit between the known and the obscure becomes penetrable, and the unremarkable turns into a material for the phenomenal.

The figure of the Tooth Pixie, whether portrayed as a brilliant sprite or a heavenly watchman, turns into a sign of the widespread human craving for wizardry. In the youngster's psyche, the Tooth Pixie rises above the constraints of the substantial, epitomizing the fanciful notion and ponder that characterize the enchantment of experience growing up. The baffling trade, organized by this ethereal figure, turns into a course for the kid's confidence in the remarkable — a conviction that, in its effortlessness, repeats the immortal longing for charm.

As the night unfurls and the trade happens, the kid stirs to the revelation of a fortune left in the stead of the minuscule tooth. This fortune, whether a glimmering coin or a knickknack permeated with representative importance, turns into a substantial badge of the concealed wizardry that unfolded during the nighttime hours. The trade turns into a token of correspondence, a quiet affirmation of the youngster's readiness to embrace the baffling and the enchanted.

The imagery inborn in the trade reaches out past the prompt delight of getting a fortune. It turns into an illustration for the transient idea of life as a youngster — a brief second when the passing of a tooth addresses actual development as well as a stage toward the domain of development. The fortune left by the Tooth Pixie turns into a remembrance, an unmistakable indication of the blamelessness that once graced the youngster's grin.

Social varieties in the act of "The Puzzling Trade" add profundity to the story, uncovering the different manners by which social orders have woven their extraordinary strings into this widespread embroidery. Whether through customary customs, stylized acts, or neighborhood folklores, the trade turns into a material onto which social qualities and convictions are painted. These varieties, instead of weakening the pith of the practice, add to its wealth and versatility across geological and social scenes.

In diving into the verifiable underlying foundations of the baffling trade, one experiences old traditions and convictions that rise above time. The idea of trading a lost tooth for a badge of significant worth has reverberations in the fables of different civic establishments. From old Norse legends to social practices in various districts, the demonstration of putting importance on lost teeth turns into a string that interfaces different stories of human experience.

The figurative reverberation of "The Secretive Trade" likewise reaches out to the close to home territory of growing up. The kid, in leaving behind a tooth, goes through an unobtrusive yet significant change — an excursion set apart by the blending of energy, sentimentality, and an expanding consciousness of the progression of time. The Tooth Pixie, as the quiet observer to these profound subtleties, turns into a buddy in the kid's journey from honesty to encounter.

In the contemporary setting, the puzzling trade experiences the flows of advancement, mixing antiquated customs with the mechanical scenes of the 21st hundred years. Messages to the Tooth Pixie, computerized messages, and virtual trades become present day emphasess of this deep rooted practice. However, underneath the facade of mechanical progressions, the pith of the trade continues — a festival of miracle, conviction, and the persevering through enchantment settled in the core of experience growing up.

As the story attracts to a nearby, "The Baffling Trade: Tooth for a Fortune" arises not just as an interesting youth custom but rather as an immortal articulation of mankind's journey for enchantment and significance. A story rises above the limits of culture and time, welcoming every age to participate in the charm that exists in the normal. In the straightforwardness of a lost tooth and the fortunes left afterward, the baffling trade turns into an immortal sign of the fragile dance between the substantial and the elusive, the known and the obscure — a dance that unfurls in the tranquil spaces where the enchantment of life as a youngster flourishes and blooms.

Chapter 4

The Language of Smiles

In the tremendous range of human articulation, the language of grins arises as a general and nuanced type of correspondence that rises above social, phonetic, and topographical limits. The demonstration of grinning, an apparently straightforward facial motion, conveys significant importance for of conveying feelings, building associations, and exploring the many-sided embroidery of human collaborations. As we dive into the rich scene of "The Language of Grins," we reveal the complex elements of this nonverbal language — a language that says a lot in its nuance and comprehensiveness.

The Comprehensiveness of Grins:

At its center, the language of grins is general, a common code that resounds across societies and social orders. Despite etymological contrasts, a grin can connect holes, produce associations, and discuss feelings with a lucidity that rises above words. The comprehensiveness of grins highlights the natural human limit with respect to compassion and understanding, certifying that, in the domain of feelings, a grin is a language that everybody fathoms.

The Facial Symphony:

The human face, enhanced with bunch looks, turns into a material for the facial ensemble that is the language of grins. From the unobtrusive upswing of the lips to the crinkling of the eyes, every subtlety adds to the ensemble of feelings. A real grin, frequently portrayed by the initiation of facial muscles around the eyes, transmits warmth and credibility. This coordination of looks fills in as a nonverbal exchange, a quiet discussion that unfurls in the common spaces between people.

Social Varieties in Grins:

While the substance of a grin is all inclusive, social subtleties shape the significance and translation of this nonverbal articulation. In certain societies, a grin might imply consideration or a token of understanding, while in others, it might convey warmth, cordiality, or even humiliation. Understanding the social setting in which a grin happens adds layers of profundity to the language, uncovering the mind boggling dance between individual articulation and cultural standards.

The Developmental Underlying foundations of Grinning:

The language of grins is well established in human development, filling in as an endurance component and an instrument for social holding. Babies, from the earliest transformative phases, display grins for the purpose of correspondence with guardians, laying out an establishment for social association. As people experienced, the capability of grins reaches out past fundamental correspondence, turning into a nuanced instrument for exploring the intricacies of human connections.

The Life systems of a Grin:

Past its mental and social aspects, the life systems of a grin divulges the complicated transaction of muscles, nerves, and feelings. The Duchenne grin, named after the French nervous system specialist Duchenne de Boulogne, is portrayed by the enactment of both the zygomatic significant muscles (which raise the edges of the mouth) and the orbicularis oculi muscles (which crease the eyes). This certifiable, full-confronted grin is frequently connected with true certain feelings.

Close to home Reverberation:

The language of grins fills in as a conductor for profound reverberation, permitting people to convey euphoria, satisfaction, entertainment, and a bunch of good sentiments. A grin has the ability to elevate spirits, make a feeling of fellowship, and diffuse pressure in relational communications. Whether traded between companions, outsiders, or across social partitions, a certified grin turns into a widespread cash of generosity.

The Cryptic Idea of Sneers and Grins:

In the huge collection of grins, the baffling idea of sneers and unpretentious grins adds a charming layer to the language. A sneer, portrayed by a half-grin or a guileful articulation, can pass a scope of feelings — from entertainment on to self-assuredness. These nuanced articulations frequently welcome translation, featuring the many-sided dance among straightforwardness and hidden significance inside the language of grins.

Grins in Friendly Elements:

In friendly elements, grins become social ointments, facilitating the progression of correspondence and cultivating a feeling of association. A grin can go about as a greeting, flagging receptiveness and congeniality. In social scenes, shared grins make a feeling of solidarity and shared insight, building up friendly bonds. The correspondence of grins in friendly trades frames an implicit arrangement, recognizing the common space of collaboration.

The Force of Sympathy:

At its pith, the language of grins is a strong vehicle for compassion. An empathetic grin, stretched out in snapshots of happiness or distress, imparts understanding and shared feeling. The capacity to identify grins shapes the establishment for strong connections, cultivating a feeling of having a place and close to home reverberation. In the midst of festivity or misfortune, a grin turns into a quiet confirmation of shared human encounters.

Exploring Proficient Fields:

In proficient fields, the language of grins takes on nuanced aspects. An expert grin, portrayed by an equilibrium between warmth and convention, is a significant device for building compatibility and laying out a positive impression. Whether in conferences, meets, or systems administration occasions, a very much coordinated and certifiable grin can convey receptiveness, certainty, and impressive skill.

Grins in Sentiment and Closeness:

In issues of sentiment and closeness, the language of grins turns into a dance of shared feelings and implicit association. The coy grin, the bashful grin, or the friendly grin all add to the multifaceted movement of heartfelt communications. Grins in these settings act as a language of want, enthusiasm, and the implicit articulations of adoration.

Grins as Ways of dealing with stress:

Despite misfortune, the language of grins frequently arises as a survival technique. The flexibility implanted in a grin, even in testing conditions, mirrors the human ability to track down strength in weakness. A rebellious grin can be a demonstration of opposition, a refusal to be characterized by difficulty, and a certification of the unyielding soul inside.

The Grin Body Association:

Past its effect on profound prosperity, the language of grins is unpredictably connected to actual wellbeing. The demonstration of grinning triggers the arrival of endorphins, synapses that add to sensations of bliss and prosperity. This brain body association highlights the helpful capability of grins in advancing mental and profound wellbeing.

Computerized Grins in the Virtual Domain:

In the period of computerized correspondence, the language of grins reaches out into virtual spaces. Emojis and emoticons, graphical portrayals of looks, act as advanced grins that improve online cooperations. These viewable signs become essential to conveying tone, state of mind, and feelings in message based correspondence, overcoming any barrier made by the shortfall of actual presence.

Grins Across Ages:

As overseers of social coherence, the language of grins rises above ages, connecting the youthful and the old in a common story of human experience. The upbeat grins of kids, imbued with guiltlessness and richness, summon grins from seniors who witness the unrestrained energy of youth. In this transaction, the language of grins turns into an immortal string that winds through the texture of familial and cultural bonds.

Grins as Thoughtful gestures:

Thoughtful gestures, frequently appeared through grins, have the ability to make waves of energy on the planet. A straightforward grin stretched out to a more peculiar, a partner, or a bystander can light up somebody's day and make a chain response of generosity. The language of grins, in these occurrences, turns into an impetus for cultivating a feeling of local area and interconnectedness.

Challenges in Translation:

In spite of its comprehensiveness, the language of grins isn't without its difficulties in understanding. Social subtleties, individual contrasts, and setting assume essential parts in molding the significance of a grin. A grin that conveys warmth in one culture might be seen as held in another. Exploring these nuances requires a nuanced comprehension of the different manners by which grins are communicated and deciphered.

Grins in Craftsmanship and Imagination:

The language of grins tracks down articulation in craftsmanship and imagination, filling in as a dream for specialists, scholars, and makers. Visual portrayals of grins catch the quintessence of human feelings, from the Mona Lisa's cryptic grin to scholarly depictions that inspire the glow of a person's grin. In the domain of imagination, grins become a material for narrating, feeling, and the investigation of the human mind.

The Social Effect of Grins:

On a cultural level, the aggregate effect of grins is significant. Public spaces decorated with grins, whether as open craftsmanship, local area occasions, or shared snapshots of satisfaction, add to a positive and comprehensive social climate. Grins, as an aggregate articulation, become impetuses for encouraging a feeling of solidarity and shared humankind.

The Grin in the Mirror:

The most private experience with the language of grins happens in the reflection gazing back from the mirror. The independent grin, whether conceived out of self-acknowledgment, confidence, or a snapshot of individual victory, holds extraordinary power. The grin in the mirror turns into a reflection of the spirit, mirroring the interior scene of feelings and the excursion toward self-revelation.

Grins In the midst of Affliction:

Maybe the most piercing part of the language of grins is its strength in the midst of misfortune. The capacity to track down comfort, strength, and even snapshots of delight amidst difficulties addresses the unstoppable soul inside. Grins, at these times, become a demonstration of the human ability to explore haziness with a flash of light — an update that, even in difficulty, the language of grins can be an encouraging sign.

The Implicit Obligation of Shared Grins:

In the quiet trades of shared grins, a remarkable bond is produced — an implicit comprehension that rises above words. Whether between companions, relatives, or outsiders, the language of grins turns into an extension that traverses the holes of language, culture, and individual contrasts. In these common minutes, the force of human association is refined into a basic, yet significant, articulation.

Grins as Influencers:

In the domain of social change and activism, the language of grins fills in as a specialist of change. Aggregate grins become encouraging signs, energizing networks toward shared objectives. Grins, whether despite misfortune or chasing after equity, epitomize the soul of strength and the enduring confidence in the chance of positive change.

The Getting through Tradition of Grins:

As we explore the complicated territory of human communications, the persevering through tradition of grins turns into a demonstration of the versatility of the human soul. From the support to advanced age, the language of grins goes with people on their excursion, making a permanent imprint on the common story of humankind. In the straightforwardness of a grin, we track down an immortal articulation of bliss, association, and the general language that ties every one of us.

In closing our investigation of "The Language of Grins," we end up drenched in an embroidery woven with strings of feeling, association, and the common human experience. From the certifiable warmth of a sincere grin to the cryptic articulations that welcome understanding, the language of grins rises above the limits of language and culture. A language addresses the center of our common mankind, advising us that, in the ensemble of human articulation, a grin stays a widespread tune — a challenge to interface, to comprehend, and to commend the significant excellence intrinsic in the straightforward demonstration of turning up the edges of our lips. As we convey the tradition of grins into the future, may each common grin become a demonstration of the getting through force of human association and the endless limit with regards to delight that dwells inside every one of us.

4.1. Communicating through Grins

In the tremendous and complicated scene of human correspondence, there exists a special and generally figured out type of articulation — the language of smiles. This nonverbal language, portrayed by the unobtrusive shape of lips and the fun loving nature of facial muscles, rises above etymological hindrances to convey a range of feelings, goals, and shared encounters. As we set out on an investigation of "Conveying through Smiles," we dive into the multi-layered elements of this expressive structure — a language that unfurls in the unconstrained, the purposeful, and the perplexing smiles traded in the embroidery of human connections.

The Immediacy of Smiles:

At the core of imparting through smiles lies a component of suddenness — a certifiable, unscripted reaction to snapshots of delight, entertainment, or association.

Unconstrained smiles, frequently joined by a sparkle in the eyes, catch the substance of a common encounter, whether it be an entertaining comment, a magnificent shock, or a startling association. At these times, smiles become an instinctive articulation of the delight that penetrates the present, making a common space of joy among people.

The Perkiness of Sneers:

Inside the language of smiles, the grin arises as an energetic and quietly devilish articulation. A grin, described by an incomplete and frequently unbalanced grin, passes a scope of feelings — from entertainment on to self-assuredness. The perkiness innate in grins welcomes understanding, adding a component of interest to the nonverbal trade. This nuanced type of correspondence fills in as a material for communicating mind, certainty, or a common perspective between people.

The Subtleties of Unexpected Smiles:

Unexpected smiles acquaint a layer of intricacy with the language, conveying a feeling of mockery, doubt, or a fun loving affirmation of incongruity. The unobtrusive lift of one corner of the mouth, joined by a knowing look, conveys a message that reaches out past the strict significance of words. Amusing smiles become instruments for exploring the complicated territory of mind, humor, and the common acknowledgment of the idiocies woven into the texture of regular day to day existence.

Smiles as Bonds in Shared Minutes:

In shared snapshots of happiness or win, smiles act as bonds that associate people in the festival of common encounters. Whether in the result of a common accomplishment, the seeing of an endearing scene, or the zenith of an aggregate exertion, smiles become an aggregate articulation of bliss. In these cases, the language of smiles turns into a binding together power, meshing people into a common story of delight and kinship.

Exploring Social Elements with Smiles:

The language of smiles assumes a pivotal part in exploring social elements, offering people a device for communicating friendliness, receptiveness, and transparency. A cordial smile, described by warmth and truthfulness, turns into an encouragement to participate in friendly connections. The capacity to decipher and answer meaningful gestures passed on through smiles adds to the ease of relational connections, encouraging a feeling of association and mutual perspective.

The Puzzling Force of Baffling Smiles:

Puzzling smiles, set apart by a baffling and cryptic quality, enrapture the creative mind and welcome interest. These smiles, frequently described by an unobtrusive slant of the head or a flicker in the eyes, pass on a feeling of kept data or a perky feeling of secret. The cryptic force of these smiles lies in their capacity to provoke curiosity, welcoming the people who experience them to dig further into the layers of significance and goal.

Social Varieties in Smiling:

While the language of smiles rises above social limits, there exist social varieties in the understanding and articulation of smiles. In certain societies, smiling might be related with good manners, understanding, or a well disposed disposition. In others, the impression of smiles might be impacted by social standards encompassing looks and close to home presentation. Understanding these social subtleties adds profundity to the language of smiles, accentuating the significance of setting and social mindfulness in nonverbal correspondence.

Smiles as Strategies for dealing with stress:

Despite misfortune or difficulties, smiles frequently arise as survival strategies, mirroring the versatility and strength of the human soul. The rebellious smile, portrayed not entirely set in stone and hopeful articulation, turns into a useful asset for confronting troubles with a funny bone and enduring purpose. Smiles, in these examples, act as a demonstration of the ability to track down daintiness amidst dimness.

Smiles in Proficient Fields:

In proficient fields, the language of smiles takes on nuanced aspects, filling in as a device for exploring the intricacies of working environment connections. The expert smile, portrayed by a harmony between cordiality and custom, turns into a resource in building compatibility, diffusing strain, and encouraging positive work environment elements. The purposeful utilization of smiles in proficient settings mirrors a comprehension of the effect of nonverbal correspondence on proficient connections.

Smiles as Articulations of Warmth:

Inside the domain of individual connections, smiles act as articulations of warmth, closeness, and shared euphoria. The private smile traded between significant others, the pleased smile of a parent seeing a kid's accomplishment, or the certifiable smile divided among dear companions all add to the close to home wealth of unique interactions. Smiles, in these specific situations, become a language of adoration, care, and shared encounters.

The Nuances of Smothered Smiles:

Smothered smiles, set apart by an endeavor to disguise or control a grin, add a captivating layer to the language of smiles. These smiles might arise in circumstances where people try to keep a cool head in conventional settings or stifle chuckling in unseemly minutes. The unpretentious play between a stifled smile and the eyes uncovers the fragile harmony between keeping up with decency and surrendering to the irresistible idea of happiness.

Smiles in Thoughtful gestures:

Thoughtful gestures, whether as some assistance, an act of kindness, or a real commendation, frequently inspire thankful smiles. The correspondence of thoughtfulness and the subsequent smiles make a positive input circle, adding to a common feeling of generosity and interconnectedness. Smiles become visual insistences of the effect of thoughtfulness on both the provider and the beneficiary.

Advanced Smiles in the Virtual Domain:

In the time of advanced correspondence, the language of smiles stretches out into virtual spaces through emoticons and emojis. Computerized smiles, passed on through visual images, improve online connections by giving a visual portrayal of the shipper's close to home tone. The energetic winks, the wide smiles, and the devilish sneers in the advanced domain become present day cycles of nonverbal correspondence, associating people across virtual distances.

Smiles Across Ages:

The language of smiles, as an immortal type of articulation, rises above generational partitions, connecting people across various age bunches in a common language of bliss and entertainment. The irresistible idea of smiles, particularly with regards to shared chuckling, makes spans between the youthful and the old, encouraging a feeling of intergenerational association. In the trading of smiles, the congruity of human encounters unfurls across the embroidery of ages.

The Mending Force of Giggling and Smiles:

Giggling, frequently joined by irresistible smiles, has a significant mending power. The remedial advantages of giggling, both physical and mental, add to generally speaking prosperity. Shared snapshots of giggling and smiles make bonds, mitigate pressure, and act as remedys to the difficulties of life. The mending force of smiles reaches out past the individual, impacting aggregate prosperity and encouraging a feeling of local area.

Smiles as Specialists of Positive Change:

In the domain of cultural effect, smiles arise as specialists of positive change. Aggregate smiles, communicated in snapshots of shared win, festivities, or thoughtful gestures, add to a positive and comprehensive social climate. Smiles become impetuses for encouraging a feeling of solidarity, separating hindrances, and motivating people to take part in activities that add to the improvement of society.

The Implicit Figuring out in Friendly Smiles:

Friendly smiles, traded between people who share a profound comprehension and association, rise above the requirement for verbal correspondence. These smiles impart kinship, shared encounters, and a quiet affirmation of the connection between companions, relatives, or partners. In helpful smiles, the implicit language turns into a demonstration of the strength of connections based on common comprehension.

The Philosophical Underpinnings of Smiles:

Rationally, the language of smiles welcomes consideration on the idea of euphoria, humor, and the fleeting idea of human encounters. Smiles, as momentary articulations of enjoyment, help people to remember the fleetingness of minutes and the significance of relishing the delight innate in the present. The philosophical underpinnings of smiles support a careful hug of the wealth tracked down in shared giggling and articulations of bliss.

Smiles in Workmanship and Imagination:

The language of smiles tracks down articulation in workmanship, writing, and imaginative undertakings, turning into a wellspring of motivation for specialists and makers. Visual portrayals of smiles catch the range of human feelings, from the capricious to the significant. Scholarly depictions of characters' smiles add to the nuanced depiction of characters and the investigation of close to home scenes in imaginative works.

Smiles as Reflectors of Internal States:

Past the outside articulations, smiles act as reflectors of inward states and profound scenes. The unpretentious varieties in the curve of lips, the force of the look, and the general disposition during a smile give bits of knowledge into the profound condition of people. Along these lines, smiles become mirrors that mirror the inward delights, difficulties, and subtleties of the human mind.

Exploring Incongruity and Mind Through Smiles:

The language of smiles assumes a significant part in exploring incongruity and mind, offering people a material for communicating humor and keenness. Unexpected smiles, matched with a knowing look, convey a common acknowledgment of the disjointed qualities or idiocies in a circumstance. Smiles become instruments for injecting discussions with levity, testing points of view, and exploring the intricacies of mind.

The Tradition of Smiles:

As we close our investigation of "Imparting through Smiles," we are left with the acknowledgment that smiles structure a permanent heritage in the common human account. From unconstrained articulations of delight to purposeful demonstrations of correspondence, the language of smiles typifies the dynamic quality, variety, and interconnectedness of the human experience. Whether traded in snapshots of win, challenges, or regular collaborations, smiles rise above words to become immortal articulations of the delight, chuckling, and shared associations that weave the texture of our aggregate process. In the tradition of smiles, we find a persevering through festival of the human soul and the significant magnificence implanted in the straightforward demonstration of grinning.

4.2. Toddler's toothy smiles as a form of expression

In the magnificent scene of youth, toddlerhood arises as an eccentric stage set apart by vast interest, investigation, and the rise of energetic grins that act as charming types of articulation. As we leave on an investigation of "Baby's Energetic Grins as a Type of Demeanor," we dive into the nuanced aspects of these charming smiles, revealing the importance, formative achievements, and the sheer delight implanted in the excited grins that embellish the essences of little children.

The Imagery of the Main Tooth:

The appearance of a little child's most memorable bite denotes a critical formative achievement, frequently joined by an outpouring of excited grins that enlighten their countenances. The imagery inborn in the development of that small, magnificent tooth stretches out past the actual demonstration of getting teeth. It turns into a substantial signifier of development, both as far as actual turn of events and the unfurling excursion of youth. The main tooth, looking through sensitive gums, proclaims the progress from sticky smiles to the enchanting presentation of a baby's energetic grin.

The Cheerful Articulation of Disclosure:

Toddlerhood is a period of perpetual investigation — a period set apart by the sheer pleasure of finding their general surroundings. The energetic grin turns into a cheerful articulation of newly discovered revelations, whether it be the adventure of getting a handle on an item interestingly, the energy of making those shaky first strides, or the charm of drawing in with brilliant toys. Each excited smile catches the quintessence of the baby's endless interest and the sheer euphoria got from the demonstration of investigation.

Correspondence through Grins:

Well before babies ace the complexities of verbal language, they impart through a language of grins. The excited smile fills in as an incredible asset for nonverbal correspondence, permitting babies to convey a range of feelings — from pleasure and entertainment to love and satisfaction. Guardians, parental figures, and relatives become proficient at translating the subtleties of these excited grins, laying out an exceptional type of correspondence that rises above words.

The Improvement of Social Bonds:

Energetic grins assume a critical part in the improvement of social bonds during the baby years. As little children connect with guardians, kin, and friends, their excited smiles become solicitations to participate in equal play and shared encounters. The infectious idea of these grins makes a positive input circle, cultivating a feeling of association and supporting the connections between the little child and their social climate. The excited smile, in its irresistible satisfaction, turns into a social paste that ties people in snapshots of shared joy.

Articulations of Solace and Security:

In the safe hug of a parental figure or the commonality of a valued climate, babies frequently express their solace and feeling that everything is good through brilliant excited grins. These grins become consolations, confirming the baby's confidence in their guardians and the security of their environmental elements. The excited smile, joined by a glimmer of acknowledgment, conveys a significant feeling of satisfaction and the fundamental conviction that they are cherished, really focused on, and safeguarded.

Exploring Difficulties with Flexibility:

Toddlerhood, in spite of its glad minutes, isn't without its difficulties. From getting teeth uneasiness to the dissatisfaction of unfulfilled cravings, babies experience a scope of feelings that track down articulation in their excited grins. These smiles, versatile notwithstanding minor difficulties, become markers of the little child's ability to explore difficulties with a feeling of flexibility. The energetic grin, even in the midst of snapshots of trouble, turns into a visual demonstration of the innate confidence that portrays youth.

The Job of Creative mind and Play:

Creative mind blooms during the little child years, and energetic grins frequently go with the eccentric universes made through play. Whether participated in creative play with toys, investigating the domains of pretend, or delighting in the delight of narrating, babies express their inventive undertakings through brilliant smiles. The energetic grin turns into a passage to the mysterious scenes that unfurl inside the rich embroidery of a baby's creative mind.

Energetic Smiles as Profound Indicators:

The nuances of a little child's excited smile act as close to home indicators, offering bits of knowledge into their internal world. A naughty smile might flag an energetic plan, while a timid grin might mirror a snapshot of vulnerability or faltering. By intently noticing these excited articulations, guardians and parental figures gain important signals about the baby's personal state, permitting them to answer with awareness and backing to the consistently changing scene of toddlerhood.

Social Meaning of Grins:

The social meaning of energetic grins in toddlerhood differs across social orders, yet generally, the delight exuding from these smiles rises above social limits. In certain societies, the development of a little child's most memorable tooth is praised as a representative transitional experience, set apart by customs and customs. The energetic grin turns into a public wellspring of bliss, welcoming more distant family and local area individuals to partake in the joy of the baby's formative achievements.

Parental Pride and Shared Grins:

For guardians, seeing their little child's energetic smile turns into a wellspring of inconceivable unrivaled delight. These grins, frequently joined by chuckling and richness, summon a feeling of satisfaction in seeing the development and bliss of their kid. Divided grins among guardians and babies structure a strong bond, making a repository of positive feelings that reinforce the parent-youngster relationship. The excited smile, caught in valued minutes, turns into an enduring engraving on the hearts of guardians.

Energetic Grins in Instructive Settings:

In instructive settings, the language of energetic grins assumes a crucial part in encouraging positive early growth opportunities. Instructors and parental figures, receptive to the expressive idea of little children, utilize these smiles as marks of commitment, interest, and close to home prosperity. Establishing a climate that sustains excited grins includes consolidating euphoric exercises, intuitive learning, and potential open doors for socialization, guaranteeing that the early instructive excursion is set apart by a feeling of bliss and energy.

Visual Souvenirs of Toddlerhood:

Guardians frequently anxiously catch the energetic smiles of their babies through photos, changing these grins into appreciated remembrances that embody the quintessence of youth. Photograph collections loaded up with pictures of energetic grins become visual accounts, archiving the development, achievements, and the sheer extravagance of toddlerhood. These visual fortunes act as immortal tokens of a passing yet otherworldly part in the kid's excursion.

The Change from Sticky Smiles to Full Dentition:

As little children progress through the phases of youth, the excited grins that once exhibited a solitary tooth develop into presentations of full dentition. The change from sticky smiles to a bunch of teeth denotes a groundbreaking period in dental turn of events. The energetic smile, presently embellished with an assortment of teeth, turns into a demonstration of the regular movement of development and the rise of the kid's interesting grin.

Dentition as Markers of Distinction:

The singularity of a baby's excited grin stretches out past the simple presence of teeth — it turns into an unmistakable component that adds character and uniqueness. Varieties in tooth arrangement, dispersing, and the planning of tooth ejection add to the customized appeal of every kid's grin. The excited smile, with its peculiarities, turns into a marker of the little child's developing character and a wellspring of charm for the people who love them.

Keeping up with Oral Wellbeing and Sustaining Grins:

As babies embrace the excursion of dental turn of events, guardians assume a pivotal part in keeping up with oral wellbeing and supporting those valuable grins. Presenting great oral cleanliness rehearses, for example, delicate tooth brushing and customary dental check-ups, turns into an establishment for deep rooted dental prosperity. The demonstration of really focusing on a little child's teeth stretches out past the actual parts of dental cleanliness — it typifies the obligation to safeguarding the wellbeing and brilliance of their excited smiles.

Excited Grins in Playgroups and Socialization:

In playgroups and group environments, excited grins become basic to the elements of little child socialization. The trading of smiles between babies during play encourages associations, advances shared pleasure, and lays the foundation for the improvement of interactive abilities. The excited grin, frequently joined by giggling and shared play encounters, adds to the development of early kinships and the upbeat investigation of the social world.

Adapting to Getting teeth Uneasiness:

Getting teeth, a characteristic piece of dental turn of events, can at times carry inconvenience to little children. The energetic smiles that persevere through getting teeth act as versatile appearances even with gentle uneasiness. Guardians and parental figures, sensitive to the indications of getting teeth, offer calming measures and solace to lighten any related distress. The energetic grin, even in the midst of the difficulties of getting teeth, mirrors the baby's ability to explore actual uneasiness with a feeling of determination.

The Charming Idea of Hole Toothed Grins:

As babies change to the period of blended dentition, the development of hole toothed grins adds a charming quality to their smiles. These enchanting holes, frequently brief as grown-up teeth continuously arise, add to the interesting and lovable nature of the baby's grin. The energetic smile, with its perky defects, turns into a visual demonstration of the transient and unconventional nature of youth.

Observing Achievements with Energetic Smiles:

As little children arrive at formative achievements, from their initial steps to the expression of beginning words, excited smiles become celebratory markers of accomplishment. The delight communicated through these grins intensifies the meaning of every achievement, making an embroidery of excited smiles that intersperse the excursion of youth. Guardians and parental figures, seeing these achievements, participate in the sheer joy reflected in the energetic grins of their little children.

Energetic Smiles as Profound Anchors:

In snapshots of close to home disturbance, energetic smiles frequently arise as profound anchors for babies. Whether despite minor misfortunes, short lived disappointments, or snapshots of vulnerability, the encouraging idea of an energetic grin turns into a self-relieving instrument. The demonstration of grinning, in any event, during testing minutes, mirrors the baby's natural capacity to track down happiness and profound soundness inside themselves.

Catching the Substance of Blamelessness:

Energetic grins in toddlerhood epitomize the pith of honesty — an unfiltered, certified articulation of satisfaction unburdened by cultural assumptions. These grins emanate virtue, earnestness, and an unrestrained excitement forever. In the effortlessness of an energetic smile, spectators get looks at the clean satisfaction that characterizes the early long periods of life as a youngster, helping everybody to remember the excellence inborn in honesty.

Energetic Grins as Valuable Recollections:

As little children progress into adolescence and then some, the energetic grins that once embellished their countenances become valuable recollections appreciated by guardians, relatives, and parental figures. These recollections, carved in the heart, persevere as tokens of when excited smiles enlightened the ordinary snapshots of happiness, chuckling, and disclosure. The demonstration of reviewing those energetic grins turns into a nostalgic excursion back to the sorcery and miracle of toddlerhood.

In finishing up our investigation of "Baby's Energetic Grins as a Type of Articulation," we end up drenched in the captivating universe of youth — a domain where excited smiles act as brilliant articulations of satisfaction, interest, and the unfathomable enchantment of honesty. From the imagery of the main tooth to the festival of formative achievements, each energetic grin turns into a remarkable brushstroke on the material of a baby's excursion.

These smiles, rising above words and social limits, convey the all inclusive language of delight that characterizes the quintessence of toddlerhood. As we praise the excited grins that effortlessness the essences of babies, we commend the persevering through magnificence of experience growing up — the unadulterated, unfiltered happiness that leaves a permanent engraving on the hearts of all who witness it.

4.3. Parental decoding of baby talk

In the mind boggling dance of early parent-youngster correspondence, the peculiarity of "child talk" arises as a nuanced type of collaboration that rises above the regular limits of language. This charming practice includes guardians adjusting their discourse examples, pitches, and jargon while speaking with their newborn children. As we dig into the investigation of "Parental Disentangling of Child Talk," we unwind the complex layers of this novel correspondence style, revealing insight into its importance, the formative effect on babies, and the natural deciphering process attempted by guardians.

The Musicality of Child Talk:

Child talk, frequently portrayed by its sing-tune quality, melodic rhythm, and overstated inflections, makes a phonetic song that catches the consideration of babies. Guardians intuitively mix their discourse with musicality, as though creating a customized cradlesong, perceiving that the cadenced and apparent components of child talk draw in the baby's hear-able faculties. The musicality innate in child talk rises above phonetic semantics, shaping a scaffold that associates parent and kid through the common language of tune.

Semantic Disentanglement and Redundancy:

At the center of child talk lies the specialty of etymological improvement. Guardians normally smooth out their discourse by utilizing more limited sentences, worked on jargon, and tedious expressing. This deliberate improvement fills numerous needs — it helps with catching the newborn child's consideration, works with appreciation through redundancy, and lays the basis for language securing. Through the monotonous idea of child talk, babies start to observe examples and affiliations, cultivating the beginning phases of language understanding.

Profound Reverberation in Newborn child Coordinated Discourse:

Past its semantic viewpoints, child talk is implanted with profound reverberation that frames a vital part of parent-baby holding. The glow, fondness, and delicacy implanted in baby coordinated discourse add to the production of a protected profound climate. Guardians, receptive to the feelings of their newborn children, instinctively mix their words with adoration and solace. The close to home shapes of child talk become a channel through which guardians impart data, yet additionally a profound feeling of care and association.

Reflect Neurons and Mimicry:

The unraveling of child talk by guardians includes an interesting transaction of mirror neurons and mimicry. As guardians notice their babies' prompts, articulations, and endeavors at vocalization, reflect neurons in the parental cerebrum are actuated. This neurological reaction prompts guardians to reflect their babies' sounds and articulations intuitively. Through this proportional mimicry, a non-verbal discourse unfurls, making a powerful trade where guardians and newborn children co-make the interesting language of their relationship.

Building Starting points for Language Obtaining:

Child talk, a long way from being a simple phonetic variation, fills in as a platform for the baby's initial language securing. The improved on grammar, monotonous designs, and misrepresented pitches intrinsic in child talk furnish babies with a language structure that lines up with their mental limits. Guardians, going about as etymological aides, establish the groundworks for their babies' language improvement by naturally taking care of the mental and hear-able necessities of the creating mind.

Joint Consideration and Correspondence Advancement:

Parental interpreting of child talk includes a complex comprehension of joint consideration — the common spotlight among parent and baby on a specific item, motion, or sound. Through the cadenced and connecting with nature of child talk, guardians cultivate joint consideration minutes that become urgent for correspondence improvement. Newborn children, brought into the common phonetic trade, figure out how to connect sounds with articles and ideas, starting the many-sided dance of shared consideration that underlies powerful correspondence.

Social Varieties in Child Talk:

While the embodiment of child talk is widespread in its plan to draw in and speak with babies, social varieties impact the particular subtleties of this training. Various societies might display unmistakable ways to deal with child talk, remembering varieties for pitch, inflection examples, and, surprisingly, the decision of explicit sounds or words. Social disentangling of child talk includes a transformation of these subtleties, mirroring the rich embroidery of social impacts on early parent-baby correspondence.

The Job of Nonverbal Prompts:

Deciphering child talk reaches out past the domain of expressed words — it includes a significant comprehension of nonverbal prompts traded among parent and baby. Looks, eye to eye connection, non-verbal communication, and motions become vital parts of the interpreting system. Guardians, finely sensitive to their newborn children's nonverbal signs, explore the rich scene of child talk by consolidating a comprehensive methodology that embraces both verbal and nonverbal components.

Parental Instinct and Responsiveness:

Parental unraveling of child talk is, at its substance, an instinctive interaction directed by a profound aversion to the requirements and reactions of the baby. This instinctive interpreting includes a complementary dance where guardians answer their babies' vocalizations, articulations, and motions with an adjusted responsiveness. The parental sense to change discourse designs, tweak tone, and give ameliorating reactions mirrors a natural comprehension of the mind boggling signals implanted in the rich embroidery of child talk.

The Powerful Idea of Child Talk:

As newborn children progress through various formative stages, the unique idea of child talk turns out to be progressively clear. Guardians, skilled at unraveling their newborn children's advancing necessities, change their correspondence styles likewise. From the early coos and jabbering of earliest stages to the development of first words and the beginning of expressive motions, child talk adjusts to line up with the unfurling mental and phonetic limits of the developing kid. The powerful idea of child talk reflects the steadily changing scene of youth advancement.

Corresponding Communication and Turn-Taking:

Deciphering child talk includes a consciousness of the equal idea of parent-baby connection. Turn-taking, a key part of viable correspondence, is instinctively woven into the texture of child talk. Guardians, sensitive to the rhythms of their newborn children's reactions, make a conversational stream set apart by substituting vocalizations, stops, and shared articulations. This turn-taking unique cultivates a feeling of conversational correspondence, laying the foundation for the newborn child's future language creation.

Mental Advantages of Child Talk:

Past its close to home and etymological aspects, the disentangling of child talk by guardians assumes an essential part in encouraging mental advantages for babies. The rich hear-able excitement gave through misrepresented pitches and cadenced examples adds to the improvement of hear-able handling abilities. Furthermore, the monotonous idea of child talk supports design acknowledgment and the foundation of brain associations that structure the reason for future language and mental capacities.

Individual Varieties in Parental Child Talk:

Each parent carries an extraordinary flavor to the disentangling of child talk, prompting individual varieties in correspondence styles. These varieties might be impacted by private encounters, social foundations, and the extraordinary parent-baby bond. A few guardians may normally incline toward perky and enlivened child talk, while others might take on a more mitigating and delicate tone. The variety in parental child talk styles features the wealth of individual articulation inside the more extensive system of this charming correspondence practice.

Advances to Conversational Discourse:

As newborn children progress through the phases of youth, the disentangling of child talk bit by bit changes into additional mind boggling types of conversational discourse. The basic components laid through child talk act as building blocks for the kid's language improvement. Guardians, sensitive to their kid's arising phonetic capacities, explore this change by continuously consolidating a more extensive jargon, more complicated sentence structures, and empowering the youngster's dynamic support in discussions.

Parental Responsiveness and Connection:

Disentangling child talk includes a major part of parental responsiveness — the capacity to adjust to the baby's signs and answer in an ideal and strong way. This responsiveness shapes the bedrock of secure connection among parent and baby. Through the mindful translating of child talk, guardians lay out an informative bond that rises above words, making a safe close to home establishment that supports the youngster's socio-personal turn of events.

Adjusting Child Converse with Individual Babies:

Parental deciphering of child talk is certainly not a one-size-fits-all undertaking; rather, it includes a perfect versatility to the extraordinary necessities and disposition of individual babies. Guardians, finely receptive to their newborn children's inclinations, change the pitch, beat, and content of child converse with line up with the particular signs and reactions of every youngster. This customized variation mirrors the cozy comprehension guardians create as they explore the multifaceted scene of their newborn children's correspondence styles.

The Continuum of Language Advancement:

Translating child talk fills in as a passage to the continuum of language improvement that unfurls as babies change into babies and then some. The central components laid out through child talk become the venturing stones for the procurement of jargon, sentence structure, and the subtleties of expressive language. The unraveling system advances close by the youngster's semantic excursion, incorporating the happy rise of first words, the investigation of language through play, and the improvement of conversational abilities.

Praising the Delight of Correspondence:

As guardians participate in the deciphering of child talk, there is a festival of the delight innate in the common snapshots of correspondence. The giggling, the energized trades, and the common have a great time the dance of words make an energetic embroidery of shared satisfaction. At these times, the embodiment of child talk rises above the details of language procurement — it turns into a festival of the significant happiness that emerges from the personal correspondence among parent and baby.

In finishing up our investigation of "Parental Deciphering of Child Talk," we wind up drenched in the charming domain of early parent-baby correspondence. Child talk, with its melodic rhythm, close to home reverberation, and versatility, turns into a language of adoration that rises above the limits of verbal articulation. The interpreting system embraced by guardians mirrors a finely tuned attunement to the necessities, signals, and developing limits of their newborn children. As guardians explore the mind boggling scene of child talk, they establish the ground-works for language advancement as well as manufacture obligations of association and connection that persevere all through the excursion of life as a youngster. In the embroidery of early correspondence, the translating of child talk remains as a demonstration of the significant magnificence of the common language of affection among guardians and their babies — a language that rises above words and reverberates with the immortal tune of parental consideration and dedication.

Chapter 5

Gentle Beginnings

In the sensitive embroidery of life, the idea of "Delicate Starting points" winds around a story that rises above the limits of time, exemplifying the nuanced substance of beginning over again, leaving on excursions, and embracing the unfurling parts of presence. As we leave on an investigation of Delicate Starting points, we dig into the complex layers of this suggestive topic, disentangling its importance across different parts of human experience.

The Beginning of Another Day:

Delicate starting points frequently track down their figurative sign in the appearance of another day. The main beams of daylight puncture the obscurity, providing reason to feel ambiguous about a brilliant gleam the world. This everyday ceremonial fills in as a delicate update that each sunrise carries with it the commitment of reestablishment, offering a chance to begin once more. In the tranquil snapshots of dawn, people track down comfort and motivation, embracing the figurative day break as an image of trust, flexibility, and the vast potential outcomes that lie ahead.

Birth and the Wonder of Life:

One of the most significant appearances of delicate starting points is seen in the wonder of birth. The appearance of an infant into the world denotes the inception of an excursion loaded up with commitment, potential, and the delicate hug of new life. From the main cries that reverberation in the conveyance space to the fragile elements of the newborn child, birth represents a delicate initiation — a pivotal starting that proclaims the beginning of a singular's remarkable story in the great embroidery of presence.

The Murmurs of Nature:

Nature, in its quiet excellence, frequently fills in as a material for delicate starting points. The unpretentious spreading out of a bloom's petals, the development of delicate shoots from the dirt, or the sensitive rippling of a butterfly's wings —

all typify the beauty and quietness inborn in the normal world. These murmurs of nature resound with the tranquil force of delicate starting points, helping spectators to remember the repetitive idea of life, development, and resurrection.

The Initial Part of Connections:

Delicate starting points stretch out to the domain of human associations, especially in the initial parts of connections. Whether it be the provisional first discussions between people, the common chuckling of new companions, or the blooming of heartfelt love, the initiation of connections conveys the sign of tenderness. It includes a fragile dance of shared disclosure, trust-building, and the continuous interlacing of lives as people leave on the excursion of fashioning significant associations.

Instructive Odyssey and Expectations to learn and adapt:

Chasing information and self-improvement, the instructive excursion unfurls as a progression of delicate starting points. From the principal day of school, where wide-looked at understudies step into the domain of the scholarly world, to the beginning of advanced education and professional pursuits, each stage addresses another section in the book of learning. The delicate starting points in schooling envelop the obtaining of information as well as the improvement of decisive reasoning, versatility, and the molding of one's character from the perspective of learning.

Imaginative Beginning and Inventive Investigations:

Imagination, in its horde structures, frequently tracks down its beginning in delicate starting points. The primary strokes of a painter's brush on a fresh start, the initial notes of a performer's sythesis, or the underlying words wrote by an essayist — all mean the initiation of creative undertakings. The inventive flow unfurls tenderly, permitting craftsmen to investigate, explore, and rejuvenate their creative dreams. In the domain of imaginative articulation, delicate starting points make ready for the advancement of show-stoppers.

Vocation Adventures and Expert Spearheading:

Proficient excursions reflect the topic of delicate starting points as people step onto the way of vocation adventures. The main day at a new position, the commencement into a picked calling, or the send off of an enterprising undertaking — all address snapshots of beginning in the expert circle. These starting points are set apart by a mix of fervor, fear, and the potential for development, as people explore the scene of their picked vocations.

Careful Advances and Individual Changes:

Delicate starting points reach out past outside achievements to incorporate the domain of individual changes. Careful changes, whether incited by self-reflection, groundbreaking encounters, or purposeful decisions, mean a cognizant inception into another period of self-awareness. These snapshots of reflection and reestablishment act as impetuses for people to reclassify their ways, embrace positive changes, and set out on an excursion of self-revelation.

Social Festivals and Ceremonial Initiations:

Social customs and festivities frequently integrate the subject of delicate starting points. Customs encompassing births, weddings, and other huge life altering situations represent the beginning of new parts inside the setting of social and cultural structures. These services, set apart by imagery, soul changing experiences, and collective interest, highlight the significance of recognizing and regarding the delicate starting points woven into the texture of shared social encounters.

Mending and Restoration after Difficulty:

In the consequence of affliction, delicate starting points manifest as strong specialists of recuperating and reestablishment. People confronting difficulties, mishaps, or snapshots of misery frequently find comfort in the possibility of beginning again. The strength implanted in the human soul considers the delicate rising up out of the shadows of difficulty, embracing trust, and remaking a feeling of direction and prosperity.

Natural Supportability and Eco-cognizant Drives:

Delicate starting points stretch out their impact to the worldwide stage, especially in the domain of natural maintainability. Drives focused on preservation, biological reclamation, and eco-cognizant living address an aggregate obligation to starting positive change for the planet. The cognizant decisions made by people, networks, and associations connote a delicate yet strong beginning of endeavors to protect the World's regular magnificence for people in the future.

Wellbeing and Health: The Craft of Taking care of oneself:

Delicate starting points track down reverberation in the domain of wellbeing and health, where the craft of taking care of oneself turns into a groundbreaking excursion. The choice to embrace better way of life rehearses, focus on mental prosperity, or set out on a wellness routine denotes the delicate inception into a way of self-supporting. These deliberate starting points, energized by self-empathy and a promise to prosperity, unfurl as a course of individual revival and imperativeness.

Parental Supporting and Youth:

With regards to life as a parent, delicate starting points unfurl as guardians leave on the supporting excursion with their youngsters. From the principal snapshots of embracing an infant to directing babies through the beginning phases of improvement, guardians become designers of delicate starting points. The delicate consideration, unqualified love, and careful nurturing rehearses shape the essential long stretches of a youngster's life, encouraging a climate where the seeds of development are planted.

The Dance of Seasons and Repetitive Recharging:

Nature, with its repetitive examples, offers a significant impression of delicate starting points through the evolving seasons. The blooming of spring, the glow of summer, the groundbreaking shades of harvest time, and the calm reflection of winter — all connote the repetitive reestablishment intrinsic in the dance of seasons. Each season delivers a delicate initiation, offering a cadenced sign of the everlasting pattern of development, torpidity, and resurrection.

Computerized Age and Mechanical Advancements:
In the period of fast mechanical progressions, delicate starting points manifest in the domain of development and advanced advancement. The send off of earth shattering advances, the inception of new companies, and the presentation of clever thoughts address the delicate beginning of groundbreaking changes in the computerized scene. Pioneers and visionaries explore unfamiliar domains, introducing another period set apart by innovative leap forwards and perspective changes.

Profound Investigations and Internal Excursions:
For some people, the way of profound investigation unfurls as an excursion of delicate starting points. The mission for internal importance, self-revelation, and association with the extraordinary addresses an individual inception into the domains of otherworldliness. Practices like contemplation, care, and thoughtful reflections become doors to a more profound comprehension of oneself and the universe, denoting the beginning of significant inward excursions.

Culinary Undertakings and Gastronomic Revelations:
Delicate starting points find articulation in the culinary domain as people leave on gastronomic
experiences and culinary investigations. The principal endeavors at cooking another recipe, the inception into assorted foods, and the production of culinary joys represent the delicate beginning of luxurious excursions. Through the craft of cooking and gastronomy, people find the delight of trial and error, flavor, and the tangible joys of the culinary world.

Abstract Drives and Imaginative Stories:
In the realm of writing and human expression, delicate starting points unfurl as scholars, craftsmen, and creatives leave on the most common way of narrating and imaginative articulation. The principal strokes of a pen on clear paper, the commencement of a novel, or the initial notes of a melodic structure connote the inception of imaginative stories. Through writing and artistic expression, people catch the pith of their encounters, creating stories that reverberate with the general subjects of life's delicate starting points.

Social Developments and Backing Drives:
The aggregate goals for social change and equity frequently start with delicate starting points inside the system of social developments and backing drives. The choice to bring issues to light, challenge cultural standards, and champion the privileges of minimized networks addresses a cognizant commencement into the domain of activism. These developments, set apart by grassroots endeavors and

local area commitment, mean the delicate yet impressive initiation of tries to make an additional fair and simply world.

Methods of Care and Present Living:

Practices of care, established in the way of thinking of living right now, typify the substance of delicate starting points. Careful living includes the cognizant commencement into the act of being completely present, developing mindfulness, and embracing every second with a feeling of receptiveness. The strategies of care, including contemplation and careful breathing, act as entryways to a condition of delicate mindfulness, where people draw in with life in a conscious and purposeful way.

Exploring Life Advances and Junction:

Delicate starting points unfurl amidst life's advances and junction. Whether set apart by changes in profession, migration to new spots, or changes in private connections, these minutes address the beginning of another stage. People explore the intersection of existence with a mix of thoughtfulness, flexibility, and the boldness to embrace the obscure, changing changes into open doors for development and self-restoration.

The Force of Little Thoughtful gestures:

The delicate starting points of positive change frequently live in the force of little thoughtful gestures. Sympathetic signals, articulations of sympathy, and the expansion of some assistance to others connote the commencement of positive waves in the aggregate human experience. The combined effect of these little demonstrations adds to the making of a more humane and interconnected world, denoting the delicate beginning of a culture of thoughtfulness.

Parental Direction and Mentorship:

In the domains of direction and mentorship, delicate starting points manifest as guardians and tutors start the most common way of supporting and significantly shaping the existences of those under their consideration. Guardians, as the main aides in a kid's life, give the primary help to development and improvement. Essentially, tutors, whether in instructive, expert, or individual circles, assume a significant part in directing people through the beginning phases of their excursions.

Magnanimity and Philanthropic Drives:

The magnanimous undertakings and philanthropic drives embraced by people and associations encapsulate the soul of delicate starting points chasing social great. The choice to add to worthy missions, start local area undertakings, or promoter for worldwide issues denotes the beginning of endeavors to have a beneficial outcome on society. Through charity, people become impetuses for groundbreaking change, starting a pattern of sympathy and liberality.

The Insight of Maturing and Intelligent Initiations:

In the later phases of life, delicate starting points take on an intelligent and pensive quality. The insight earned through long stretches of encounters turns into a wellspring of direction and knowledge. Maturing people frequently set out on an excursion of reflection, denoting a delicate beginning into a period of life portrayed by a more profound comprehension of self, a feeling of satisfaction, and the enthusiasm for life's persevering through excellence.

In closing our investigation of "Delicate Starting points," we end up drenched in the rich woven artwork of human experience, where each feature of life is moved by the delicate commencement of new parts. From the introduction of a youngster to the initiation of instructive excursions, from the unfurling of imaginative undertakings to the careful hug of present living, delicate starting points implant existence with a feeling of restoration, trust, and probability. This subject rises above transient limits, reverberating through the ages as a widespread theme that addresses the strength, flexibility, and intrinsic innovativeness of the human soul.

As people explore the bunch delicate starting points woven into the texture of their lives, they become designers of their predeterminations, creating stories that resound with the immortal rhythms of restoration and development. Whether in the individual circle of connections and self-revelation, the public field of social practices and social developments, or the broad scenes of nature and worldwide drives, delicate starting points act as the strings that tight spot people to the consistently unfurling story of presence.

In the calm snapshots of first light, the delicate spreading out of a blossom, the initiation of a sincere discussion, or the commencement of positive change, the subject of delicate starting points welcomes people to embrace existence with a feeling of receptiveness and interest. It coaxes them to perceive the excellence innate in every snapshot of beginning, producing a way of direction, association, and the persistent reestablishment of the human soul. In the ensemble of life, where each note denotes the start of another tune, the subject of delicate starting points reverberates as an immortal tribute to the persevering through limit with regards to development, change, and the unfathomable potential outcomes that anticipate the people who leave on the excursion of residing.

5.1. Nurturing the Milk Teeth

Sustaining the milk teeth is a sensitive dance between the consideration of guardians, the interest of babies, and the mind boggling organic cycles that unfurl in the beginning phases of experience growing up. The milk teeth, otherwise called deciduous or child teeth, act as the underlying set that prepares for the extremely durable teeth to follow. In this investigation of "Sustaining the Milk Teeth," we dig into the multi-layered components of really focusing on these valuable early associates, taking into account the physiological perspectives, oral cleanliness rehearses, formative achievements, and the profound scene that goes with this basic phase of dental prosperity.

The Meaning of Milk Teeth:

Milk teeth, in spite of their transient nature, assume a significant part in the general improvement of a youngster. These underlying arrangement of teeth act as placeholders for the long-lasting teeth, directing their legitimate arrangement as the kid develops. Past their utilitarian job in biting and talking, milk teeth add to facial turn of events, guaranteeing the suitable spaces and designs are saved for the approaching super durable teeth. Understanding the meaning of milk teeth highlights the significance of supporting them with care and consideration.

Dental Advancement in Youth:

The excursion of dental improvement in youth is an entrancing cycle set apart by particular stages. The emission of the primary tooth, normally close to a half year old enough, proclaims the beginning of dental achievements. As the deciduous teeth arise individually, guardians witness the development of their youngster's grin. The example of emission, the shedding of milk teeth, and the resulting appearance of long-lasting teeth structure a powerful story that unfurls through-out experience growing up. Supporting the milk teeth turns into a cooperative exertion between guardians, parental figures, and dental experts to guarantee the consistent movement of dental turn of events.

Oral Cleanliness Practices for Little children:

Laying out oral cleanliness rehearses from the little child years establishes the groundwork for a long period of dental prosperity. The presentation of tooth brushing, commonly with a delicate shuddered brush and a smear of fluoride toothpaste, turns into a custom that guardians embrace in a joint effort with their babies. The delicate cleaning of milk teeth tends to quick oral cleanliness needs as well as develops solid propensities that will serve the kid all through their life. Picking age-proper oral consideration items and ingraining the significance of normal brushing add to the comprehensive consideration of milk teeth.

Getting teeth: An Achievement and a Test:

The getting teeth ease denotes a critical achievement in a baby's dental process, yet it likewise presents difficulties for the two guardians and the youngster. The rise of new teeth can bring inconvenience, peevishness, and an inclination to bite on objects. Understanding the indications of getting teeth permits guardians to give fitting relieving measures, whether through getting teeth toys, chilled therapeutic rings, or delicate back rubs of the gums. The getting teeth experience features the requirement for responsiveness and mindfulness in supporting the kid through this period of dental turn of events.

Dietary Decisions and Their Effect:

Dietary decisions during the early years straightforwardly affect the soundness of milk teeth. An even eating regimen that incorporates fundamental supplements, especially calcium and vitamin D, upholds the improvement of solid and sound teeth. Restricting sweet bites and drinks diminishes the gamble of dental depressions and advances generally speaking oral wellbeing. Guardians assume a urgent part in directing their babies toward dietary decisions that support their developing bodies as well as add to the versatility and imperativeness of their milk teeth.

Preventive Measures and Standard Dental Check-ups:

Preventive dental consideration measures are vital to supporting the soundness of milk teeth. Dental experts prescribe the utilization of effective fluoride to reinforce tooth finish and the utilization of dental sealants to safeguard weak regions from rot. Normal dental check-ups, beginning from the emission of the principal tooth, give an open door to early discovery of any issues and consider opportune intercessions. Laying out a positive connection among little children and dental visits cultivates an underpinning of solace and confidence in dental consideration.

The Close to home Scene of Dental Consideration:

Exploring the close to home scene of dental consideration for babies includes perceiving and tending to the extraordinary difficulties and fears related with dental visits. Dental nervousness, normal among the two kids and grown-ups, can be relieved through a delicate and consoling methodology. Establishing a positive and strong climate during dental arrangements, integrating components of play and schooling, and recognizing the kid's feelings add to building a sound profound starting point for dental consideration.

Change from Milk Teeth to Extremely durable Teeth:

The change from milk teeth to super durable teeth is a characteristic movement in dental turn of events. As the kid develops, the underlying foundations of milk teeth resorb, clearing a path for the extremely durable teeth to eject. This stage, frequently joined by the shedding of milk teeth, addresses a powerful second in the youngster's excursion toward youth. Guardians, seeing this change, assume a part in directing their youngsters through the profound parts of expressing farewell to their child teeth and embracing the appearance of their super durable set.

Social Viewpoints on Dental Consideration:

Dental consideration rehearses are affected by social viewpoints, customs, and convictions. Social varieties might appear in the planning of dental consideration commencement, the kinds of oral cleanliness rehearses embraced, and the customs related with dental achievements. Understanding the social setting permits dental experts to tailor their direction to line up with the qualities and inclinations of assorted networks. Social responsiveness in dental consideration guarantees that the supporting of milk teeth is drawn nearer with deference for individual and shared points of view.

Computerized Devices and Instructive Assets:

In the time of computerized data, instructive assets and intuitive devices become significant resources in sustaining the milk teeth. Guardians approach an abundance of online assets, applications, and instructive materials that give bits of knowledge into dental consideration works on, getting teeth cures, and age-proper oral cleanliness strategies. Utilizing computerized devices as instructive guides adds to engaging guardians with information and encouraging a proactive way to deal with supporting their youngsters' dental wellbeing.

Showing Oral Cleanliness Propensities: A Long lasting Gift:

Showing oral cleanliness propensities from the early years is a long lasting gift that guardians bestow to their kids. The foundation of a steady oral consideration routine turns into a day to day custom that reaches out past youth into pre-adulthood and adulthood. The propensities ingrained during the sustaining of milk teeth act as a layout for deep rooted dental health. Enabling kids with the information and abilities to really focus on their oral wellbeing adds to the counteraction of dental issues and the advancement of in general prosperity.

Ecological Variables and Oral Wellbeing Variations:

Supporting the milk teeth includes perceiving and addressing ecological variables that add to oral wellbeing incongruities. Financial circumstances, admittance to medical services, and local area assets assume a part in deciding the oral wellbeing results of youngsters. Drives pointed toward lessening oral wellbeing variations include local area based approaches, backing for open dental consideration, and instructive projects that enable families with the apparatuses to focus on dental wellbeing, independent of their financial status.

The Job of Parental Model:

Guardians act as the essential powerhouses in forming the oral wellbeing ways of behaving of their kids. The model set by guardians, both as far as their own oral cleanliness rehearses and their perspectives toward dental consideration, altogether influences the propensities created by their kids. Displaying positive ways of behaving, showing the significance of customary dental check-ups, and cultivating a climate where dental consideration is esteemed add to making a tradition of oral wellbeing cognizance inside the family.

Mechanical Advancements in Pediatric Dentistry:

Mechanical advancements in pediatric dentistry improve the apparatuses and approaches accessible for sustaining the milk teeth. High level imaging innovations, negligibly intrusive treatment choices, and the reconciliation of computerized stages add to a complete and kid cordial dental experience. Mechanical developments work with early conclusion and intercession as well as add to making a positive and drawing in environment inside dental facilities for youthful patients.

Worldwide Drives for Pediatric Oral Wellbeing:

On a worldwide scale, drives for pediatric oral wellbeing mean to address the assorted difficulties looked by kids in changed districts. Cooperative endeavors between state run administrations, non-benefit associations, and dental experts look to carry out preventive projects, increment admittance to dental consideration, and bring issues to light about the significance of supporting the milk teeth. Worldwide drives perceive the interconnectedness of oral wellbeing with generally speaking prosperity and underscore the job of early mediations in forming the future oral soundness of networks.

In finishing up our investigation of "Sustaining the Milk Teeth," we perceive the complex embroidered artwork woven by guardians, parental figures, dental experts, and networks in encouraging the prosperity of kids during the central long periods of dental turn of events. The meaning of milk teeth reaches out past their actual capability, including close to home, social, and long lasting aspects. From the development of the principal tooth to the progress to super durable teeth, each stage addresses a section in the advancing story of a kid's oral wellbeing.

Supporting the milk teeth includes an agreeable mix of preventive measures, instructive drives, social responsiveness, and the mix of mechanical progressions. The profound scene of dental consideration, set apart by the delicate snapshots of getting teeth and the temporary stages, highlights the significance of an all encompassing methodology that thinks about the multi-faceted parts of a kid's prosperity.

As guardians and networks hold hands with dental experts in the common undertaking of supporting the milk teeth, they add to laying the basis for a future where kids develop with sound grins and an uplifting perspective toward oral wellbeing. The examples granted, propensities developed, and social subtleties regarded during the early long stretches of dental consideration reverberate as persevering through gifts that reverberation all through a kid's lifetime. In the aggregate endeavors to sustain the milk teeth, we embrace a pledge to the prosperity of the future, cultivating a tradition of grins that reflect the strength of teeth as well as the delight and certainty that go with a long period of good oral wellbeing.

5.2. Dental care for toddlers

Dental consideration for little children is a pivotal part of their general prosperity, establishing the groundwork for a long period of sound oral propensities. The early long periods of a youngster's life are set apart by huge achievements in dental turn of events, from the emission of the principal tooth to the change to a full arrangement of super durable teeth. In this extensive investigation of "Dental Consideration for Babies," we dig into the diverse components of oral wellbeing for small kids, enveloping preventive measures, age-fitting oral cleanliness rehearses, dietary contemplations, the profound scene of dental consideration, and the co-operative job of guardians and dental experts in cultivating ideal dental wellbeing.

The Rise of Essential Teeth:

The excursion of dental consideration for little children starts with the rise of essential teeth, otherwise called deciduous or child teeth. This interaction commonly starts close to a half year old enough when the main tooth shows up. The ejection of essential teeth is a dynamic and consecutive cycle, with every tooth assuming a particular part in the youngster's oral turn of events. Understanding the timetable of tooth emission permits guardians and parental figures to expect and address the particular necessities related with each stage.

Early Dental Cleanliness Practices:

Laying out early dental cleanliness rehearses is essential to the general consideration of baby's teeth. Indeed, even before the ejection of the main tooth, guardians can start oral consideration by delicately cleaning the child's gums with a perfect, moist fabric. As teeth arise, the progress to a delicate seethed toothbrush and a smear of fluoride toothpaste becomes fundamental. Acquainting little children with the idea of tooth brushing in a perky and positive way makes way for deep rooted oral cleanliness propensities.

Age-Fitting Toothpaste and Toothbrush Choice:

Choosing age-fitting toothpaste and toothbrushes is a vital thought in dental consideration for little children. Pediatric toothpaste with a lower fluoride focus is prescribed for small kids to forestall the gamble of fluorosis while as yet giving the advantages of fluoride in forestalling tooth rot. Delicate seethed toothbrushes intended for little children guarantee delicate cleaning without making harm arising teeth and touchy gums.

Showing Legitimate Tooth-Brushing Procedures:

Showing little children legitimate tooth-brushing procedures includes a progressive and patient methodology. Guardians can show others how its done, exhibiting the right movements and empowering little children to impersonate. The utilization of drawing in toothbrushes with lively tones or most loved characters can make the experience more charming. Underlining the significance of arriving at all surfaces of the teeth and advancing autonomy in tooth brushing are fundamental parts of showing legitimate procedures.

The Job of Diet in Oral Wellbeing:

Dietary decisions assume a vital part in the oral wellbeing of babies. The utilization of sweet tidbits and drinks represents a gamble for dental cavities. Guardians are urged to offer a reasonable eating regimen that incorporates organic products, vegetables, dairy items, and entire grains. Restricting the admission of sweet treats and underlining water as the essential refreshment add to the counteraction of tooth rot. The connection among's sustenance and oral wellbeing highlights the all encompassing nature of dental consideration for babies.

The Getting teeth Interaction and Mitigating Measures:

The getting teeth process, set apart by the ejection of new teeth, can be joined by uneasiness and touchiness in little children. Understanding the indications of getting teeth permits guardians to execute relieving measures to reduce inconvenience. Therapeutic rings, chilled washcloths, and delicate gum kneads give alleviation. The utilization of over-the-counter getting teeth gels or effective sedatives ought to be drawn nearer with alert, heeding the direction of medical care experts to guarantee wellbeing.

Preventive Measures: Sealants and Fluoride:

Preventive measures, like the utilization of dental sealants and fluoride, add to the insurance of little child's teeth. Dental sealants are flimsy coatings applied to the biting surfaces of molars to forestall the collection of plaque and microscopic organisms. Skin fluoride applications, either as gels, stains, or expertly controlled medicines, fortify tooth finish, lessening the gamble of cavities. The fuse of these preventive measures is an essential piece of complete dental consideration for little children.

Customary Dental Check-ups for Little children:

Starting standard dental check-ups for little children is prescribed to screen their oral wellbeing and address any arising issues expeditiously. The American Foundation of Pediatric Dentistry suggests the principal dental visit around the hour of the main tooth emission or by the kid's most memorable birthday. Early dental visits consider proficient evaluation as well as make a positive relationship among little children and dental consideration, cultivating a feeling of solace and commonality.

Tending to Youth Holes:

Youth holes, otherwise called child bottle tooth rot or youth caries, can influence babies and may prompt serious oral medical problems whenever left untreated. This condition is frequently connected with drawn out openness to sweet fluids, like milk or squeeze, particularly when little children nod off with a jug. Forestalling youth pits includes embracing practices like not permitting delayed bottle use, weakening sweet beverages, and advancing normal tooth brushing.

Fluoride Supplementation: Adjusting Advantages and Dangers:

Fluoride supplementation is a subject of thought in dental consideration for babies, especially in regions where the regular fluoride content in water is deficient. The American Dental Affiliation suggests fluoride supplementation in the wake of surveying individual gamble factors, including water fluoride levels and the youngster's age. Finding some kind of harmony between the advantages of fluoride in forestalling cavities and the gamble of fluorosis requires cooperation among guardians and dental experts.

Conduct The executives in Pediatric Dentistry:

Conduct the executives is an essential part of pediatric dentistry, particularly while managing little children. Dental experts utilize methodologies like uplifting feedback, interruption procedures, and age-fitting clarifications to establish a positive and agreeable climate for youthful patients. Laying out trust and compatibility among little children and dental experts adds to a smoother dental encounter and lays the foundation for inspirational perspectives toward oral consideration.

The Profound Scene of Dental Consideration:

Exploring the profound scene of dental consideration for little children includes perceiving and tending to the interesting feelings of dread and tensions related with dental visits. Dental tension, normal among the two kids and grown-ups, can be moderated through a delicate and consoling methodology. Establishing a positive and steady climate during dental arrangements, consolidating components of play and instruction, and recognizing the kid's feelings add to building a sound close to home starting point for dental consideration.

Orthodontic Contemplations in Youth:

Orthodontic contemplations in youth center around observing the arrangement and improvement of the teeth and jaw. While far reaching orthodontic treatment regularly starts in the juvenile years, early mediation might be suggested in unambiguous cases. Dental experts evaluate factors like chomp arrangement, jaw advancement, and the presence of propensities like thumb-sucking to distinguish any potential orthodontic issues that might profit from early mediation.

Social Points of view on Pediatric Dental Consideration:

Social viewpoints impact pediatric dental consideration works on, including convictions, customs, and familial ways to deal with oral wellbeing. Understanding and regarding social subtleties permit dental experts to tailor their direction to line up with the qualities and inclinations of assorted networks. Social ability in pediatric dental consideration guarantees that the cooperative endeavors between guardians, parental figures, and dental experts are socially delicate and comprehensive.

Mechanical Developments in Pediatric Dentistry:

Mechanical developments in pediatric dentistry improve the apparatuses and approaches accessible for the consideration of little child's teeth. High level imaging innovations, insignificantly obtrusive treatment choices, and the joining of computerized stages add to a thorough and youngster well disposed dental experience. Mechanical developments work with early determination and intercession as well as add to making a positive and drawing in air inside dental centers for youthful patients.

Parental Direction and Training: Enabling Guardians:

Parental direction and training assume a focal part in dental consideration for little children. Enabling guardians with information about legitimate oral cleanliness rehearses, dietary decisions, and preventive measures permits them to play a functioning job in the oral strength of their youngsters. Dental experts act as instructors, giving direction on age-suitable dental consideration and tending to any worries or questions guardians might have.

Cooperative Methodology: Guardians and Dental Experts:

The cooperative methodology among guardians and dental experts is fundamental in guaranteeing the extensive consideration of little child's teeth. Open correspondence, normal dental check-ups, and a common obligation to preventive measures make an organization that focuses on the oral wellbeing and prosperity of small kids. Dental experts offer direction, address concerns, and work cooperatively with guardians to make a fitted way to deal with dental consideration that lines up with the one of a kind requirements of every youngster.

Worldwide Drives for Pediatric Oral Wellbeing:

On a worldwide scale, drives for pediatric oral wellbeing plan to address the different difficulties looked by kids in changed locales. Cooperative endeavors between states, non-benefit associations, and dental experts look to execute preventive projects, increment admittance to dental consideration, and bring issues to light about the significance of early dental consideration. Worldwide drives perceive the interconnectedness of oral wellbeing with by and large prosperity and stress the job of early mediations in forming the future oral strength of networks.

Supporting Grins for a Lifetime:

In closing our investigation of "Dental Consideration for Babies," we perceive the significant effect that early dental consideration has on the general wellbeing and prosperity of small kids. The excursion from the emission of the main tooth to the progress to extremely durable teeth is set apart by achievements, difficulties, and amazing open doors for preventive measures. The cooperative endeavors of guardians, parental figures, and dental experts add to establishing a positive and strong climate that sustains the grins of little children for a lifetime.

Dental consideration for babies envelops something beyond the actual parts of oral wellbeing; it includes tending to close to home necessities, social contemplations, and the strengthening of guardians as accomplices in care.

The illustrations learned, propensities developed, and preventive estimates embraced during the early years reverberate as persevering through gifts that reverberation all through a kid's lifetime. In the aggregate undertaking to support grins for a lifetime, we embrace a promise to the prosperity of the future, encouraging a tradition of oral wellbeing cognizance that adds to a reality where each youngster can grin with certainty and delight.

5.3. Milestones in tooth development

Achievements in tooth advancement follow the captivating excursion of dental development and development from the earliest phases of outset through youth and immaturity. The cycle includes a mind boggling interchange of hereditary, organic, and natural factors that guide the development, emission, and possible substitution of teeth. This extensive investigation of "Achievements in Tooth Improvement" will explore through the ordered movement of dental occasions, revealing insight into the complexities of essential and extremely durable teeth, formative achievements, and the meaning of oral wellbeing in different phases of life.

Baby Oral Wellbeing: The Beginning of Tooth Advancement:

The excursion of tooth advancement starts in the pre-birth period, with tooth buds framing in the undeveloped stage. Notwithstanding, it is during the primary long stretches of life that the underlying achievements in tooth improvement become clear. When a newborn child arrives at the age of a half year, the essential teeth, otherwise called deciduous or child teeth, begin to emit. The lower focal incisors are many times the trailblazers in this cycle, getting through the gums and denoting the commencement of a deep rooted odontogenic venture.

Getting teeth: A Turbulent however Inescapable Achievement:

Getting teeth, a generally perceived and frequently turbulent achievement, regularly starts close to a half year old enough. The development of teeth through the gums can cause distress, crabbiness, and a characteristic tendency to bite on objects for help. This stage, while trying for the two babies and guardians, implies the continuous movement of tooth advancement. Therapeutic rings, chilled materials, and delicate gum rubs become devices for mitigating the uneasiness related with this huge achievement.

The Ejection of Essential Teeth: A Progressive Disclosing:

The ejection of essential teeth follows a distinct succession, with every tooth making its presentation in a particular request. As the lower focal incisors get through first, they are joined by the upper focal incisors, horizontal incisors, first molars, canines, and second molars in a continuous disclosing. This successive rise fills a utilitarian need, supporting the rumination of various food surfaces and laying the preparation for the inevitable progress to a blended dentition.

Blended Dentition: An Extension Among Essential and Long-lasting Teeth:

The blended dentition stage, commonly happening between the ages of six to twelve years, is set apart by the concurrence of essential and super durable teeth. The shedding of essential teeth and the emission of extremely durable teeth present a unique stage in tooth improvement. The lower focal incisors are again spearheads in this change, trailed by the upper focal incisors, parallel incisors, first molars, canines, second molars, lastly, the third molars or shrewdness teeth.

Ejection of Extremely durable Teeth: The Zenith of Dental Development:

The ejection of extremely durable teeth is a crucial achievement that reaches out from the blended dentition stage into youthfulness. As essential teeth are shed, they clear a path for the long-lasting replacements. This cycle unfurls continuously, coming full circle in the rise of the third molars, normally in the late teenagers or mid twenties. The timing and succession of long-lasting tooth emission fluctuate among people, affected by hereditary variables and generally oral wellbeing.

Orthodontic Contemplations: Exploring Tooth Arrangement:

Orthodontic contemplations become conspicuous during the blended dentition and long-lasting dentition stages. The arrangement of teeth, impediment, and nibble are basic viewpoints that might require intercession. Orthodontic appraisals assist with recognizing potential issues like malocclusions, swarming, or misalignments. Early orthodontic mediations, frequently started during the blended dentition stage, mean to direct tooth advancement and forestall or address orthodontic worries before they become more testing to make due.

Social and Ethnic Varieties in Tooth Improvement:

Tooth improvement isn't exclusively a natural interaction; it is likewise impacted by social and ethnic varieties. The planning of tooth emission, social ceremonies encompassing tooth achievements, and customary practices connected with oral wellbeing can contrast across assorted networks. Understanding and regarding these social subtleties is fundamental for dental experts, guaranteeing that oral medical services is custom fitted to line up with the qualities and inclinations of people from different foundations.

Hereditary Impacts on Tooth Improvement: Disentangling the Code:

Hereditary variables assume a pivotal part in tooth improvement, impacting viewpoints, for example, the planning of emission, tooth size, and defenselessness to specific dental circumstances. Deciphering the hereditary data connected with tooth improvement adds to a superior comprehension of varieties saw among people. Research in the field of dental hereditary qualities keeps on uncovering the mind boggling hereditary pathways that oversee tooth morphogenesis and development.

Dental Irregularities: Exploring Surprising Pathways:

While tooth improvement follows a run of the mill direction, different dental inconsistencies can modify this direction. Conditions, for example, hypodontia (missing teeth), hyperdontia (additional teeth), and dental abnormalities might introduce difficulties that require specific dental consideration. Early identification and mediation by dental experts are essential in overseeing dental abnormalities and guaranteeing ideal oral wellbeing results.

Insight Teeth: The Finish of Tooth Advancement:

The emission of third molars, regularly known as shrewdness teeth, addresses the summit of tooth improvement. This stage regularly happens in the late teenagers or mid twenties. Shrewdness teeth, named for the age at which they commonly arise, can act difficulties such like impaction, swarming, or misalignment. Observing the ejection of shrewdness teeth and resolving potential issues are fundamental parts of exhaustive dental consideration in the last phases of tooth improvement.

Dental Consideration Across the Life expectancy: A Continuum of Oral Wellbeing:

Achievements in tooth advancement are complicatedly connected to oral wellbeing across the life expectancy. From the rise of the principal tooth in earliest stages to the culmination of tooth improvement with the ejection of shrewdness teeth, oral consideration is a continuum. Ordinary dental check-ups, preventive measures, and a guarantee to oral cleanliness add to keeping up with sound teeth and gums over the course of life. The illustrations learned and propensities developed during every achievement become essential parts of a long lasting excursion towards ideal oral wellbeing.

Periodontal Wellbeing: Past Teeth to Gums and Supporting Designs:

Achievements in tooth advancement reach out past the noticeable crowns to envelop the strength of supporting designs, including gums and the periodontium. Periodontal wellbeing is vital to generally speaking oral wellbeing, and achievements in periodontal advancement include the development of supporting tissues around every tooth. The anticipation of periodontal sicknesses through successful oral cleanliness practices and standard expert cleanings is fundamental for safeguarding the life span and dependability of teeth.

Tooth Misfortune and Substitution: Exploring Advances:

Tooth misfortune, whether because of normal shedding or extractions, denotes a temporary stage in dental turn of events. The deficiency of essential teeth is a characteristic event that makes ready for the emission of long-lasting teeth. In adulthood, tooth misfortune might result from different variables, including rot, injury, or periodontal sickness. Tending to tooth misfortune includes contemplations of utilitarian and tasteful substitutions, like dental inserts, extensions, or false teeth.

Worldwide Viewpoints on Oral Wellbeing: Tending to Abberations:

Achievements in tooth advancement happen inside the setting of worldwide differences in oral wellbeing. Admittance to dental consideration, preventive measures, and consciousness of oral wellbeing rehearses differ across locales and networks. Worldwide drives plan to address these variations, stressing the significance of oral wellbeing as a basic part of in general prosperity. Cooperative endeavors between states, associations, and medical care experts try to further develop oral wellbeing results and diminish imbalances around the world.

Mechanical Advances in Dentistry: Molding the Fate of Tooth Improvement:

Mechanical advances in dentistry add to forming the fate of tooth improvement. From computerized imaging and symptomatic devices to creative treatment modalities, innovation assumes a critical part in upgrading dental consideration. Negligibly obtrusive procedures, accuracy in orthodontic mediations, and headways in materials for supportive dentistry are among the key regions where innovation impacts the direction of tooth improvement.

A Long lasting Excursion in Tooth Improvement:

In closing our investigation of "Achievements in Tooth Improvement," we perceive the multifaceted and dynamic nature of the dental excursion that traverses a lifetime. From the ejection of the main tooth to the finishing of shrewdness teeth, every achievement addresses a section in the developing story of oral wellbeing. The exchange of natural, hereditary, and ecological variables, combined with social impacts and mechanical progressions, makes a rich embroidery of variety in tooth improvement.

Understanding and valuing the meaning of every achievement in tooth advancement is central for people, guardians, and dental experts the same. The illustrations got the hang of during the developmental phases of oral wellbeing, the preventive measures embraced, and the cooperative endeavors in addressing difficulties add to forming a future where oral wellbeing is focused on across the life expectancy. In embracing the continuum of tooth improvement, we explore changes, commend accomplishments, and encourage a pledge to a long period of sound grins.

Chapter 6

Ivory Keepsakes

Ivory Remembrances, with its rich history and immortal class, has become inseparable from the craft of safeguarding recollections in stunning structure. As one digs into the complexities of Ivory Remembrances, it becomes obvious that this isn't just an organization; it is a guardian of valued minutes, a maestro of craftsmanship, and an overseer of feelings.

At the core of Ivory Souvenirs lies a guarantee to greatness that rises above ages. Laid out with a dream to exemplify the momentary magnificence of life's achievements, the organization has developed into a stronghold of creativity and refinement. The actual pith of Ivory Mementos lies in its capacity to change the normal into the phenomenal, giving lastingness to short lived minutes in time.

The specialty of creating ivory remembrances is a fragile dance among custom and development. Ivory, with its immortal allure and smooth surface, has been an image of extravagance and refinement since the beginning of time. However, Ivory Souvenirs raises this well established material higher than ever, mixing customary methods with present day plan sensibilities. The outcome is an assortment of souvenirs that stand as demonstrations of the past as well as reverberate with contemporary style.

One can't talk about Ivory Remembrances without recognizing the talented craftsmans who revive every creation. These experts, with their deft hands and faithful devotion, change crude ivory into masterpieces that recount stories without expressing a word. The careful scrupulousness is unmistakable in each bend, each form, and each unobtrusive subtlety of the completed remembrances.

The item scope of Ivory Remembrances is pretty much as different as the range of human encounters it means to epitomize. From complicatedly cut puppets that catch the quintessence of adoration to custom tailored gems pieces that honor achievements, every thing is a demonstration of the flexibility of ivory as a medium. The capacity to modify these remembrances further guarantees that every creation is just about as extraordinary as the second it addresses.

The excursion of an Ivory Souvenir starts with the choice of the best ivory. Moral contemplations are fundamental, and the organization is focused on obtaining materials dependably, complying to worldwide guidelines and advancing reasonable practices. This commitment to moral obtaining adds an additional layer of importance to every remembrance, realizing that it is created with deference for both masterfulness and the climate.

When the natural substance is chosen, the craftsmans set out on an excursion of change. The cutting system is a complex dance of accuracy and imagination. The craftsmans, frequently prepared through ages, cut multifaceted plans that mirror a profound comprehension of both the medium and the feelings they try to convey. A cycle requests persistence and veneration for the material, guaranteeing that each piece recounts to a story that is both immortal and ideal.

The plan reasoning of Ivory Mementos is an amicable mix of old style tastefulness and contemporary pizazz. Whether it's a classic enlivened memento or a cutting edge mold, the plans are permeated with a feeling of immortality. The goal isn't simply to catch a second however to rise above it, making remembrances that reverberate with the past while staying important in the present.

One of the outstanding parts of Ivory Mementos is its obligation to protecting social legacy. The organization teams up with craftsmans from assorted foundations, integrating customary themes and strategies into its plans. This not just enhances the creative woven artwork of the mementos yet additionally guarantees that social inheritances are given to people in the future. In a world that is continually developing, Ivory Souvenirs remains as a gatekeeper of legacy, meshing the strings of custom into the texture of the contemporary.

The meaning of an ivory souvenir stretches out past its tasteful allure. It is a substantial sign of elusive feelings — a scaffold between the transient and the never-ending. Whether it's a little token traded between darlings or a treasure went down through ages, every ivory memento conveys a story that rises above time. In a general public that frequently races through minutes, these mementos welcome examination, empowering people to stop and consider the significant magnificence of the encounters they epitomize.

Ivory Souvenirs, as a brand, perceives the obligation that accompanies its specialty. In a period where large scale manufacturing frequently prompts a deficiency of singularity, the organization invests wholeheartedly in making pieces that are wares as well as valued belongings. The accentuation on higher expectations without compromise is a demonstration of Ivory Mementos' obligation to making getting through relics that endure everyday hardship.

The persevering through charm of ivory as a mechanism for remembrances is a subject of examination. Ivory, with its smooth surface and warm tones, has an intrinsic delight that enraptures the viewer. A material welcomes the craftsman to investigate the constraints of innovativeness while keeping a feeling of effortlessness and refinement. The material idea of ivory adds one more aspect to the remembrances, making a tangible encounter that goes past visual feel.

As Ivory Remembrances keeps on developing, it embraces mechanical headways without compromising the quintessence of its specialty. From using state of the art cutting strategies to integrating computerized plan instruments, the organization stays at the front of development. This collaboration among custom and innovation guarantees that Ivory Tokens safeguards the past as well as expects the future, remaining significant in a powerful world.

The accounts behind Ivory Tokens are all around as different as the actual remembrances. From stories of adoration and misfortune to festivities of achievements and accomplishments, each piece has a story ready to be found. The organization, perceiving the force of these accounts, frequently teams up with its clients to mesh individual stories into tailor made manifestations. This customization adds a layer of closeness to the mementos, making them objects as well as exemplifications of individual narratives.

The cultural exchange around ivory frequently spins around moral worries and protection endeavors. Ivory Mementos, discerning of these worries, adopts a proactive strategy to address them. The organization is focused on moral obtaining, guaranteeing that the ivory utilized in its manifestations comes from lawful and supportable channels. This responsibility isn't just a demonstration of the organization's qualities yet additionally a reaction to the worldwide call for mindful and manageable practices.

The moral contemplations stretch out past the obtaining of materials to the general effect of the business on the climate. Ivory Souvenirs endeavors to limit its carbon impression, carrying out eco-accommodating practices in its creation cycles and bundling. During a time where ecological cognizance is fundamental, Ivory Mementos tries to set a model for mindful extravagance, demonstrating that impeccable craftsmanship can coincide with natural maintainability.

The social and profound meaning of ivory souvenirs is profoundly interwoven with the human experience. These antiquities, whether went down through ages or traded in snapshots of significant importance, act as unmistakable associations with our past. Ivory Mementos, with its resolute obligation to craftsmanship and narrating, arises as a watchman of these associations, guaranteeing that the tales epitomized in each piece persevere through time.

The persevering through tradition of Ivory Souvenirs is well established in its capacity to exemplify the quintessence of human feelings and encounters. Past the impeccable craftsmanship and imaginative artfulness, these tokens act as unmistakable articulations of affection, delight, and recognition. It is this significant association with the human soul that recognizes Ivory Souvenirs from simple wares, raising them to the situation with esteemed belongings with inborn worth.

The imagery of ivory, picked purposely as the mechanism for these souvenirs, adds layers of importance to every creation. Ivory has been worshipped across societies for quite a long time, implying virtue, extravagance, and an immortal delight that opposes the progression of time. Ivory Mementos, in using this valuable material, conforms to a rich custom while rethinking its motivation in the contemporary setting. The ivory utilized is a material that takes the stand concerning the tales it will convey, and the craftsmanship applied changes it into a vessel of feelings.

The excursion of an ivory token mirrors the excursion of life itself, set apart by snapshots of happiness, distress, and in the middle between. From the second a client conceptualizes a customized part of the last revealing of the carefully created memento, each step is a demonstration of the cooperative idea of the interaction. The craftsmans at Ivory Tokens invest wholeheartedly in making an interpretation of individual accounts into substantial structures, making custom tailored treasures that reverberate with the singularity of every client.

The customization cycle at Ivory Mementos is a discourse between the client and the craftsman, a dance of thoughts and motivations that come full circle in an extraordinary masterpiece. Whether it's a couple looking to deify their adoration in a couple of entwined dolls or a family celebrating an achievement through a customized design, the craftsmans approach each venture with a profound comprehension of the importance it holds. This customized touch adds profound profundity to the mementos as well as guarantees that they become treasures, went down through ages.

The close to home reverberation of Ivory Remembrances reaches out to their part in honoring life's achievements. Births, weddings, commemorations, and graduations — these crucial minutes track down a substantial structure in the painstakingly cut ivory. The mementos become vessels of memory, exemplifying the feelings, the fantasies, and the desires related with these achievements. In a world that is frequently portrayed by brevity, Ivory Remembrances stand as persevering through landmarks to the perpetual quality of adoration and accomplishment.

As gatekeepers of social legacy, Ivory Tokens perceives the significance of variety in creative articulation. The organization effectively works together with craftsmans from different social foundations, integrating conventional themes and methods into its plans. This approach not just advances the visual woven artwork of the remembrances yet in addition cultivates culturally diverse comprehension and appreciation. In a globalized world, Ivory Mementos fills in as a scaffold between different imaginative customs, making pieces that rise above social limits.

The moral contemplations encompassing the utilization of ivory have provoked worldwide discussions on protection and capable obtaining. Ivory Mementos, in exploring this complicated scene, is focused on maintaining the most noteworthy moral principles. The organization determinedly guarantees that the ivory utilized in its manifestations is obtained from lawful and manageable channels, complying to global guidelines. This responsibility not just mirrors a feeling of obligation towards the climate yet additionally sets a benchmark for moral practices inside the extravagance business.

The combination of custom and development is a sign of Ivory Mementos, clear in its plans as well as in its way to deal with craftsmanship. The craftsmans, while established in age-old methods, embrace present day apparatuses and advancements to improve their innovative flow. This agreeable mix permits Ivory Souvenirs to push the limits of what is conceivable, making remembrances that are both ageless and contemporary. The outcome is an assortment that requests to a different crowd, rising above generational and social partitions.

The material idea of ivory adds a tactile aspect to Ivory Remembrances, welcoming touch as a fundamental piece of the experience. The smooth, cleaned surfaces of the mementos ask to be held, making an unmistakable association between the item and the onlooker. This material quality upgrades the stylish allure as well as develops the close to home association, making every souvenir a sensorial excursion through the craftsmanship and the narratives it exemplifies.

In the domain of extravagance, where large scale manufacturing frequently eclipses distinction, Ivory Souvenirs remains as a signal of custom greatness. Every creation is an ongoing source of both pain and joy, a demonstration of the commitment and enthusiasm of the craftsmans who put their abilities and feelings into each piece. This obligation to higher expectations without compromise supports that genuine extravagance lies in the uniqueness and craftsmanship of every thing, rising above the transient patterns of the customer market.

Ivory Remembrances, as a brand, is mindful of its job in molding the story of extravagance. During a time where cognizant commercialization is acquiring noticeable quality, the organization's obligation to moral obtaining, ecological maintainability, and social protection positions it as a mindful player in the extravagance space. The souvenirs, with their immortal excellence and significant stories, become images of plushness as well as of a careful and intentional way to deal with extravagance.

The exchange encompassing Ivory Souvenirs reaches out past the limits of the atelier to the more extensive cultural talk on the worth of craftsmanship and significant utilization. In praising the specialty of making persevering through mementos, the organization adds to a bigger discussion on the significance of treasuring minutes and putting resources into objects that convey close to home importance. In a world immersed with efficiently manufactured products, Ivory Tokens remains as an update that genuine extravagance is tracked down in the crossing point of workmanship, feeling, and reason.

Fundamentally, Ivory Souvenirs is in excess of a brand; it is an overseer of feelings, a narrator of recollections, and a watchman of social heritages. From the customized dash of tailor made manifestations to the moral contemplations that support its practices, Ivory Remembrances epitomizes a comprehensive way to deal with the specialty of souvenir craftsmanship. As every memento finds its position in the stories of people and families, Ivory Remembrances keeps on winding around an embroidery of stories that rise above time, catching the embodiment of the human involvement with each unpredictably cut detail.

6.1. Preserving Childhood Memories

Saving cherished, lifelong recollections is a perplexing dance among sentimentality and the craft of catching brief minutes in the golden of time. As we explore the perplexing scene of growing up, there is a significant craving to exemplify the quintessence of honesty, happiness, and marvel that characterizes our initial years. The demonstration of safeguarding cherished, lifelong recollections turns into a tribute to the effortlessness and credibility that describe that developmental time of our lives.

The idea of saving lifelong recollections envelops a bunch of unmistakable and immaterial components. From actual relics like toys and photos to the vaporous feelings related with explicit encounters, the undertaking is both individual and widespread. It is an affirmation that the embroidery of our lives is woven from the strings of young life, and saving those strings is likened to defending a piece of ourselves.

Photos arise as powerful time containers in the conservation of lifelong recollections. The snap of a shade freezes a second, permitting it to rise above the limits of time. Each photo turns into an entryway to the past, opening visual subtleties as well as a surge of feelings and sensations.

The grainy surface of an old photo or the energetic shades of a very much saved preview can ship us to the universe of our life as a youngster, where consistently held the commitment of disclosure.

Past the unmistakable curios, the safeguarding of lifelong recollections frequently includes the demonstration of narrating. The oral custom of recapping stories from our childhood fills in as an extension between ages. The stories, decorated with the insight of knowing the past and the glow of shared encounters, make a familial legend that ties us to our underlying foundations. Whether it's the tale of a first bike ride or the capers of fanciful companions, the demonstration of narrating grants a feeling of progression to our own stories.

Youth is a scene painted with the dynamic tints of creative mind, and protecting those inventive domains turns into a tribute to the imaginative soul that characterizes early years. The jotted drawings, the carefully assembled craftsmanship projects, and the fantastical stories wrote in adolescent scribbling — all become curios of the uninhibited imagination that streams during youth. The cooler entryway decorated with beautiful works of art or the shoebox loaded up with manually written stories are not simply keepsakes; they are windows into the unlimited universes a youngster's brain can summon.

The safeguarding of cherished, lifelong recollections reaches out past the individual and reverberates with the shared awareness of society. Galleries committed to youth memorabilia, classic toy assortments, and displays exhibiting the development of youngsters' writing — all add to the social woven artwork of safeguarding the common experience of growing up. These arranged spaces commend the material ancient rarities of young life as well as act as tokens of the comprehensiveness of specific encounters that rise above time and social limits.

Innovation, with its tireless walk forward, has acquainted new aspects with the conservation of lifelong recollections. Computerized photograph collections, web journals, and virtual entertainment stages become current chronicles, permitting guardians to archive and share the achievements of their youngsters' lives. While these computerized archives offer accommodation and availability, they additionally bring up issues about the life span and validness of the recollections safeguarded in the advanced domain. The unmistakable idea of a photograph collection or a transcribed letter has a specific indispensable appeal that computerized configurations might battle to imitate.

The demonstration of protecting lifelong recollections is frequently interlaced with the spaces we possess. The youth home, with little hiding spots once filled in as mystery safe-houses, turns into a residing vault of recollections. Each room reverberations with giggling, tears, and the reverberations of games played in the nightfall hours. The tree in the lawn that filled in as a fort or the kitchen where the fragrance of newly heated treats waited — these spaces convey the engravings of our early stages.

As kids, our associations with toys are significant and close. The demonstration of safeguarding lifelong recollections frequently includes clutching these appreciated sidekicks. An exhausted teddy hold on for missing button eyes or a very much cherished activity figure with fight scars turns out to be in excess of a simple item; it turns into a vessel of wistfulness. The protection of these toys rises above simple sentimentality; it is a substantial connection to the feelings and connections that characterized our initial years.

Safeguarding cherished recollections is a fine art that develops as we change starting with one phase of life then onto the next. Guardians become the overseers of their kids' recollections, cautiously chronicling photos, fine arts, and written by hand notes. The demonstration of making a period case — a holder loaded up with relics of a particular second in time — turns into a purposeful undertaking to freeze a preview of experience growing up for future investigation. Opening a period case is similar to uncovering covered treasures, as the things inside convey individual importance as well as the soul of a former time.

The progression of time acquaints a powerful perspective with the safeguarding of lifelong recollections. The curios and keepsakes become demonstrations of the delights of youth as well as markers of development and change. A couple of small shoes, once worn with staggering advances, turns into an image of the excursion from outset to freedom. The protection of cherished recollections, in this unique situation, turns into a reflection on the transient idea of time and the certainty of progress.

The social and mental meaning of lifelong recollections is a subject of insightful investigation. Analysts dig into the manners by which early encounters shape character attributes, inclinations, and survival techniques. The protection of cherished, lifelong recollections, whether through helpful activities or individual reflections, turns into a device for self-disclosure and understanding. It is an affirmation that the engravings of young life keep on affecting our insights and ways of behaving long into adulthood.

In the cutting edge time, where the speed of life frequently practically rules out reflection, the demonstration of saving cherished recollections takes on a non-conformist shade. It is an intentional delay, a cognizant work to reconnect with the effortlessness and virtue of youth. The resurgence of simple photography, the ubiquity of one of a kind propelled youngsters' writing, and the recovery of exemplary toys all highlight an aggregate longing for when the world was seen from the perspective of miracle and guiltlessness.

The safeguarding of cherished recollections isn't without its difficulties. The transient idea of specific encounters, the certainty of mileage on actual antiques, and the blurring of recollections with time present obstacles to the undertaking. However, unequivocally these provokes add layers of validness to the demonstration of safeguarding. The blemishes, the frayed edges of a treasured photo, or the exhausted edges of a dearest book are not defects to be revised; they are demonstrations of the lived encounters typified inside these relics.

As we cross the scenes of adulthood, the demonstration of saving cherished, lifelong recollections turns into a conscious decision to clutch a piece of the past. It is a refusal to allow time to eradicate the impressions of youth, a promise to protecting the unadulterated and unfiltered delight that characterized our earliest years. The conservation of cherished recollections is a demonstration of affection — for oneself's purposes, for the ages that follow, and for the youngster that keeps on dwelling inside.

Protecting lifelong recollections is a continuous excursion that navigates the domains of wistfulness, sentimentality, and the specialty of epitomizing the fleeting. As we dig further into the layers of safeguarding these loved minutes, it becomes obvious that the actual demonstration is a significant reflection on the idea of time, development, and the getting through substance of honesty. The material whereupon these recollections are painted is tremendous and shifted, enveloping substantial antiques, immaterial feelings, and the spaces that act as the background to our early stages.

In the domain of unmistakable relics, photos assume a significant part in freezing minutes in time. Each photo is a part of a bigger story, a visual bookmark that permits us to return to the feelings, connections, and undertakings of our young life. The appeal of a blurred photo lies in its visual substance as well as in the tales it tells, the chuckling it catches, and the subtleties it jelly. The old photograph collection, with its yellowing pages and painstakingly organized previews, turns into a gold mine of recollections, a valued belonging went down through ages.

The demonstration of protecting lifelong recollections stretches out past the domain of photos to incorporate written by hand notes, drawings, and keepsakes. The jotted letters to guardians, the handcrafted cards for companions, and the doodles that enhanced school journals — all convey a particular appeal. These relics are more than remainders of the past; they are depictions of the imaginative soul that characterizes youth. The material idea of these items adds a tactile aspect to the demonstration of protection, as running fingers over the wrinkles of a transcribed note summons visual recollections as well as the touch and feel of a past second.

Toys, with their characteristic association with play and creative mind, become essential to the protection of cherished recollections. The battered teddy bear that filled in as a compatriot, the very much cherished doll with missing appendages, or the case of activity calculates that powered vast undertakings — all hold an extraordinary spot in the embroidery of our childhood. The choice to keep these youth sidekicks is a cognizant decision to save the actual items as well as the feelings, kinships, and inventive universes they address.

Spaces, whether physical or figurative, assume an essential part in the conservation of cherished recollections. The youth home, with its little hiding spots, turns into a residing historical center of the past. Each room conveys reverberations of giggling, tears, and the ordinary schedules that characterized our initial years.

The treehouse in the terrace, the kitchen where family dinners were shared, and the comfortable corner for sleep time stories — all become spaces permeated with the wizardry of life as a youngster. The conservation of these spaces is frequently interwoven with the demonstration of returning to, as grown-ups return to the homes of their childhood to stroll down memory paths and revive the feelings related with each space.

The demonstration of safeguarding cherished recollections takes on a familial aspect too. Guardians, as the caretakers of their kids' initial years, become dynamic members in this undertaking. From the fastidious association of photograph collections to the safeguarding of child garments and toys, guardians participate in a conscious demonstration of chronicling. The choice to report achievements, make time containers, and clutch things from each formative stage turns into a demonstration of the persevering through affection and association that characterize the parent-kid relationship.

The conservation of lifelong recollections includes a transaction between the individual and the system. While individual curios and encounters hold interesting importance, there are likewise shared social touchpoints that add to an aggregate memory of young life. One of a kind toys, exemplary kids' books, and notable kid's shows become piece of a social embroidery that rises above individual stories. Galleries committed to adolescence memorabilia and displays commending the advancement of kids' amusement become spaces where the common experience of growing up is recognized and celebrated.

Innovation, with its groundbreaking effect on the manner in which we record our lives, acquaints new aspects with the safeguarding of cherished, lifelong recollections. Computerized stages, web-based entertainment, and online photograph collections become contemporary chronicles, permitting guardians to share and archive their youngsters' achievements continuously. While these advanced arrangements offer accommodation and openness, they additionally bring up issues about the life span and legitimacy of the recollections safeguarded. The vaporous idea of advanced content, vulnerable to misfortune through innovative changes or stage out of date quality, appears differently in relation to the getting through appeal of actual antiques.

The safeguarding of cherished recollections turns into an intelligent activity as people progress starting with one phase of life then onto the next. Opening a long-neglected box of life as a youngster loves or flipping through an old photograph collection isn't just a demonstration of memory; it is a showdown with the progression of time. The items and relics, once dynamic with the energy of youth, presently convey the patina old enough. This change adds a powerful layer to the demonstration of safeguarding, as people wrestle with the double idea of time — its capacity to save and, unavoidably, to change.

In the domain of brain science, the protection of lifelong recollections takes on a restorative aspect. Analysts investigate the manners by which early encounters shape character qualities, impact direction, and add to the arrangement of personality. Drawing in with cherished recollections, whether through contemplative activities or directed remedial meetings, turns into a device for self-disclosure and recuperating. The demonstration of returning to and safeguarding these recollections fills in for of figuring out the foundations of one's convictions, fears, and yearnings.

As people cross the scenes of adulthood, the safeguarding of cherished, lifelong recollections becomes an individual undertaking as well as a social and cultural objective. In a world portrayed by fast change and consistent movement, the demonstration of esteeming the straightforwardness and credibility of experience growing up turns into a nonconformist position. The resurgence of simple photography, the fame of retro-motivated youngsters' writing, and the recovery of exemplary toys are indications of an aggregate longing for when the world was seen from the perspective of marvel and honesty.

Challenges unavoidably go with the protection of lifelong recollections. The fleeting idea of specific encounters, the mileage on actual antiques, and the blurring of recollections with time present obstacles to the undertaking. However, definitively these provokes add layers of realness to the demonstration of safeguarding. The blemishes, the frayed edges of an esteemed photo, or the exhausted edges of a cherished book are not imperfections to be rectified; they are demonstrations of the lived encounters epitomized inside these relics.

Saving cherished recollections is a multi-layered and nuanced try that rises above the person to turn into a common social and cultural story. It includes the purposeful demonstration of chronicling unmistakable relics, the close to home reverberation of spaces, and the social touchpoints that characterize an aggregate memory of life as a youngster.

Whether from the perspective of brain research, the familial setting, or the interchange between the individual and the common, the demonstration of safeguarding cherished recollections is a festival of the unadulterated, unfiltered bliss that characterizes the early long periods of life. It is a conscious decision to respect the past, love the present, and extension the ages that structure the rich embroidery of our aggregate human experience.

6.2. Creating keepsakes with fallen teeth

Making remembrances with fallen teeth is a training that rises above the standard, mixing the otherworldly domain of young life with the substantial keepsakes that demonstrate the veracity of the progression of time. The custom of losing child teeth, a soul changing experience experienced by essentially every kid, takes on added importance when these minuscule fortunes are changed into souvenirs.

This interesting and wistful practice has woven its direction into the embroidery of family customs, giving a substantial association with the short lived long stretches of life as a youngster and the charm that goes with the tooth pixie's visits.

The demonstration of gathering and making mementos from fallen teeth is a social peculiarity that traverses mainlands and ages. Guardians, grandparents, and parental figures all over the planet have, for a really long time, took part in the act of safeguarding these little, ivory-like badge of young life. The imagery connected to child teeth is rich and differed, frequently addressing the progress from earliest stages to pre-adulthood and, in many societies, connoting the youngster's excursion toward development.

One of the most well-known customs related with fallen teeth is the idea of the tooth pixie. In numerous Western societies, kids place their lost teeth under their cushions around evening time, and consequently, the tooth pixie trades the tooth for a little gift or money related reward. The unconventional charm of the tooth pixie adds a component of charm to the experience, and the souvenirs made from these fallen teeth become unmistakable tokens of the enchantment woven into the texture of young life.

In certain societies, the demonstration of losing a tooth is joined by unambiguous ceremonies or customs. For instance, in nations like Spain and a few Latin American societies, a lost tooth is put inside a glass of water on the end table. The following morning, the kid finds that the tooth has been supplanted by a little gift or a coin. These social varieties add to the rich embroidery of customs related with fallen teeth, each adding its own layer of importance to the act of making remembrances.

The tokens made from fallen teeth frequently take different structures, mirroring the imagination and wistfulness of the people who participate in this practice. One normal practice is to string the teeth into a neckband or arm band, making a novel piece of gems that epitomizes the recollections of life as a youngster. Wearing these minuscule teeth near the heart fills in as a substantial association with the temporary idea of youth, a sign of the honesty and ponder that portray early years.

Another well known approach is to encase the fallen teeth in gems settings, changing them into pendants or charms. This strategy safeguards the teeth as well as hoists them into wearable workmanship, permitting people to convey a piece of their life as a youngster with them any place they go. The craftsmanship associated with setting these small teeth into adornments adds an extra layer of creativity to the remembrances, transforming them into scaled down treasures with individual and profound importance.

For the people who lean toward a more decorative showcase, fallen teeth can be sorted out in shadow boxes or outlined close by photos, making an outwardly striking scene of cherished, lifelong recollections. This approach changes the souvenirs into ornamental pieces that can be gladly displayed in homes, filling in as ice breakers and piercing tokens of the passing idea of time.

As of late, the craft of making mementos from fallen teeth has taken a more contemporary turn with the coming of customized gems and hand crafts. Craftsmans and gem dealers team up with clients to make custom tailored pieces that grandstand the uniqueness of every tooth as well as integrate extra components, for example, birthstones or initials, to improve the wistful worth. This customized approach adds a cutting edge wind to the practice, guaranteeing that the souvenirs line up with the singular stories and inclinations of the individuals who commission them.

The nostalgic worth connected to souvenirs produced using fallen teeth reaches out past the unmistakable curios themselves. These small fortunes become vaults of recollections, typifying the giggling, tears, and development that characterize the excursion from youth to puberty. The demonstration of making souvenirs isn't only a conservation of actual remainders; it is a festival of the elusive pith of youth, an acknowledgment of the significant profound importance joined to these little, apparently unremarkable parts.

The formation of mementos from fallen teeth is a profoundly private and close cycle. Guardians, specifically, frequently wind up at the convergence of wistfulness and imagination as they set out on this excursion with their youngsters. The demonstration of gathering a tooth, cautiously putting away it, and later changing it into a remembrance turns into a common encounter that reinforces the parent-kid bond. It is a token of affection and responsibility, an unmistakable articulation of the longing to clutch the valuable minutes that get away all excessively fast.

As youngsters become older and become dynamic members all the while, the making of mementos turns into a type of narrating. Every tooth, with its remarkable shape and size, conveys its own story — a story of versatility, of developing torments, and of the inflexible walk toward development. Guardians and kids the same end up returning to these accounts, thinking back about the narratives behind each fallen tooth and the going with tooth pixie visits that additional a bit of sorcery to the common.

The wistfulness related with making mementos from fallen teeth isn't bound to a solitary social setting. Across the globe, different customs and convictions join on the common experience of young life and the widespread idea of losing child teeth. In a few Asian societies, for instance, fallen teeth are frequently covered as opposed to left for the tooth pixie, with the conviction that this act will areas of strength for guarantee sound grown-up teeth. No matter what the particular traditions, the basic subject remaining parts reliable — the affirmation that the demonstration of losing teeth is a huge and groundbreaking piece of a youngster's excursion.

The making of mementos from fallen teeth additionally crosses with the more extensive talk on memory and the manners by which people decide to remember their background. In a world immersed with computerized ephemera, the rawness of souvenirs takes on added importance. The material idea of a tooth neckband or an outlined presentation adds a tactile aspect to the demonstration of memory, permitting people to contact, feel, and associate with their past in a substantial manner.

The craft of making remembrances from fallen teeth isn't without its intricacies and questions. Some might contemplate the moral contemplations encompassing the change of human body parts, even as little as child teeth, into objects of enhancement. Others might wrestle with the idea of lastingness, contemplating whether these remembrances will persevere through time and ages or then again assuming they will, similar to youth itself, blur into the openings of memory. These inquiries add layers of examination to the work on, welcoming people to consider the idea of connection, the progression of time, and the social subtleties that shape our viewpoints.

The specialty of making tokens with fallen teeth digs into the core of experience growing up, changing the common demonstration of losing child teeth into a mysterious and wistful excursion. As a persevering through custom that traverses societies and ages, the training resounds with the widespread experience of life as a youngster, catching the substance of blamelessness and miracle. The minuscule fortunes, once painstakingly gathered and changed into remembrances, become unmistakable connections to the passing long stretches of youth, entwining with the charm of the tooth pixie's visits and the immortal stories of growing up.

In the huge scene of social works on encompassing fallen teeth, the tooth pixie stands apart as a capricious and loved figure. Across Western societies, kids fold their lost teeth underneath their cushions around evening time, anxiously expecting the tooth pixie's nighttime visit. As a trade-off for their contribution, the tooth pixie leaves a little gift or a badge of money related esteem. This wonderful trade raises the demonstration of losing teeth into an otherworldly encounter, and the fallen teeth become relics as well as keys to a domain of life as a youngster charm.

Past the Western practice of the tooth pixie, different societies overall have their interesting traditions related with losing child teeth. In Spain and a few Latin American nations, a lost tooth is much of the time put in a glass of water on the kid's end table. Before sun-up, the tooth has been supernaturally supplanted with a little gift or a coin. These different practices add to a rich embroidery of worldwide customs, each saturated with its own imagery and social importance.

The mementos molded from fallen teeth arrive in a variety of structures, mirroring the imagination and wistfulness of the people who take part in this practice. A typical practice includes hanging the teeth into neckbands or wristbands, making wearable charms that epitomize the recollections of life as a youngster. The cadenced example of teeth hung together turns into a visual portrayal of development and change, a small timetable of a kid's formative process.

Gems settings likewise give an enrapturing method for safeguarding fallen teeth, changing them into pendants or charms. The craftsmanship associated with setting these fragile teeth into adornments adds a creative aspect to the mementos, transforming them into little fortunes with both stylish and nostalgic worth. The subsequent pieces serve as decorations as well as private impressions of the wearer's very own account.

For the people who lean toward a more beautiful showcase, fallen teeth find a spot in shadow boxes or edges, frequently joined by photos or other memorabilia. This approach makes a visual scene that protects the teeth as well as fills in as a dazzling piece of craftsmanship. These showcases become central focuses in homes, starting discussions and welcoming watchers into the nostalgic universe of cherished recollections.

As of late, the well established custom of making souvenirs with fallen teeth has embraced innovation through customized and specially crafted gems. Craftsmans and goldsmiths team up with people to create customized pieces that exhibit the uniqueness of every tooth as well as consolidate extra components, for example, birthstones or initials. This contemporary methodology guarantees that the souvenirs line up with individual stories and inclinations, offering a customized and present day curve to an immortal practice.

The wistfulness appended to mementos produced using fallen teeth reaches out past the actual antiques themselves. These little fortunes become archives of recollections, typifying the chuckling, the tears, and the development that characterize the excursion from youth to puberty. The demonstration of making souvenirs isn't simply a protection of actual leftovers; it is a festival of the elusive quintessence of youth, an acknowledgment of the significant profound importance joined to these apparently ordinary parts.

Making remembrances from fallen teeth is a profoundly private and cozy cycle, frequently embraced by guardians as a team with their kids. The demonstration of gathering a tooth, putting away it with care, and later changing it into a token turns into a common encounter that fortifies the parent-youngster bond. It is a token of affection and responsibility, an unmistakable articulation of the longing to clutch the valuable minutes that get away all excessively fast.

As kids effectively take part simultaneously, the making of souvenirs turns into a type of narrating. Every tooth, with its remarkable shape and size, conveys its own story — a story of strength, of developing torments, and of the unyielding walk toward development. Guardians and kids wind up returning to these accounts, thinking back about the tales behind each fallen tooth and the captivating tooth pixie visits that additional a dash of wizardry to the standard.

The wistfulness related with making mementos from fallen teeth isn't restricted to a solitary social setting. Across the globe, different customs and convictions merge on the common experience of life as a youngster and the all inclusive nature of losing child teeth. In a few Asian societies, for instance, fallen teeth are frequently covered as opposed to left for the tooth pixie, with the conviction that this act will major areas of strength for guarantee solid grown-up teeth. No matter what the particular traditions, the hidden subject remaining parts steady — the affirmation that the demonstration of losing teeth is a critical and extraordinary piece of a youngster's excursion.

The production of souvenirs from fallen teeth converges with the more extensive talk on memory and the manners by which people decide to celebrate their background. In a world immersed with computerized ephemera, the rawness of souvenirs takes on added importance. The material idea of a tooth neckband or an outlined showcase adds a tactile aspect to the demonstration of memory, permitting people to contact, feel, and associate with their past in a substantial manner.

The act of making remembrances with fallen teeth brings up complex issues and contemplations. Moral worries might emerge as people mull over the change of human body parts, even as little as child teeth, into objects of enhancement. Some might wrestle with the idea of changelessness, contemplating whether these mementos will persevere through time and ages or on the other hand assuming that they will, similar to adolescence itself, blur into the openings of memory. These inquiries add layers of consideration to the work on, welcoming people to ponder the idea of connection, the progression of time, and the social subtleties that shape their points of view.

All in all, the formation of mementos with fallen teeth is an immortal and multi-faceted practice that epitomizes the supernatural and nostalgic parts of young life. From the fanciful notion of tooth pixie visits to the creativity engaged with making customized gems, the training is a festival of the transient idea of youth and the craving to clutch substantial tokens of these valuable minutes.

The mementos become more than simple relics; they develop into vaults of stories, feelings, and shared encounters, associating people to the charm of life as a youngster and the getting through sorcery of change. As this custom keeps on winding around its way through different societies and ages, it remains as a demonstration of the immortal longing to safeguard the quintessence of youth in substantial, getting through mementos.

6.3. The sentimental value of baby teeth

The wistful worth of child teeth rises above the rawness of these little, ivory-like fortunes, digging profound into the domains of sentimentality, familial bonds, and the mixed entry of time. The small, disposed of teeth, frequently gathered and saved by guardians or parental figures, become more than simple natural antiques — they develop into treasured mementos weighed down with close to home importance. This well established custom of esteeming child teeth mirrors an all inclusive opinion shared across societies, winding around a story of young life, development, and the getting through associations that tight spot ages.

The demonstration of gathering and loving child teeth is a social peculiarity that traverses mainlands and ages. From Western practices based on the un-conventional tooth pixie to different traditions around the world, the training is a piercing affirmation of the transient idea of life as a youngster. In numerous Western societies, youngsters enthusiastically fold their lost teeth underneath their pads, anticipating the tooth pixie's nighttime visit. The trading of teeth for little gifts or coins adds a bit of charm to the experience, and the protected teeth become remainders as well as keys to a universe of young life wizardry.

Past the Western practice, different societies have their exceptional traditions related with child teeth. In a few Asian societies, for example, the custom includes tossing lost teeth onto the rooftop or covering them to guarantee solid and sound grown-up teeth. These different practices add to a rich embroidery of world-wide customs, each permeated with its own imagery and social importance. The nostalgic worth connected to child teeth, regardless of the particular traditions, highlights a common acknowledgment of the significant excursion from earliest stages to youthfulness.

The souvenirs made from child teeth manifest in a variety of structures, mirroring the imagination and wistfulness of the people who take part in this custom. One predominant methodology includes hanging the little teeth into pieces of jewelry or wristbands, making wearable charms that epitomize the recollections of life as a youngster. The musical example of teeth hung together turns into a visual portrayal of development and change, a small scale timetable of a youngster's formative process.

Gems settings likewise give an enamoring method for saving child teeth, changing them into pendants or charms. The craftsmanship associated with setting these fragile teeth into gems adds an imaginative aspect to the mementos, transforming them into small scale treasures with both tasteful and wistful worth. The subsequent pieces serve as enhancements as well as cozy impressions of the wearer's very own story.

For the people who lean toward a more embellishing show, child teeth frequently find a spot in shadow boxes or edges, joined by photos or other memorabilia. This approach makes a visual scene that saves the teeth as well as fills in as a charming piece of workmanship. These showcases become central focuses in homes, starting discussions and welcoming watchers into the nostalgic universe of cherished, life-long recollections.

Lately, the deep rooted custom of safeguarding child teeth has embraced innovation through customized and specially crafted adornments. Craftsmans and diamond setters team up with people to create tailor made pieces that grandstand the uniqueness of every tooth as well as consolidate extra components, for example, birthstones or initials. This contemporary methodology guarantees that the remembrances line up with individual stories and inclinations, offering a customized and present day turn to an immortal practice.

The nostalgia joined to mementos produced using child teeth reaches out past the actual curios themselves. These little fortunes become stores of recollections, exemplifying the chuckling, the tears, and the development that characterize the excursion from earliest stages to pre-adulthood. The demonstration of making mementos isn't only a safeguarding of actual remainders; it is a festival of the elusive embodiment of youth, an acknowledgment of the significant close to home importance connected to these apparently unremarkable sections.

Making mementos from child teeth is a profoundly private and close cycle, frequently embraced by guardians as a team with their youngsters. The demonstration of gathering a tooth, putting away it with care, and later changing it into a souvenir turns into a common encounter that reinforces the parent-kid bond. It is a token of adoration and responsibility, an unmistakable articulation of the craving to clutch the valuable minutes that get away all excessively fast.

As youngsters effectively partake all the while, the making of remembrances turns into a type of narrating. Every tooth, with its interesting shape and size, conveys its own story — a story of versatility, of developing torments, and of the unyielding walk toward development. Guardians and kids wind up returning to these accounts, thinking back about the tales behind each fallen tooth and the captivating tooth pixie visits that additional a hint of wizardry to the conventional.

The wistfulness related with making remembrances from child teeth isn't bound to a solitary social setting. Across the globe, various customs and convictions combine on the common experience of young life and the all inclusive nature of losing child teeth. In a few Asian societies, for instance, fallen teeth are frequently covered as opposed to left for the tooth pixie, with the conviction that this act will major areas of strength for guarantee solid grown-up teeth. No matter what the particular traditions, the hidden topic stays reliable — the affirmation that the demonstration of losing teeth is a huge and groundbreaking piece of a youngster's excursion.

The making of souvenirs from child teeth likewise converges with the more extensive talk on memory and the manners by which people decide to recognize their background. In a world immersed with computerized ephemera, the rawness of mementos takes on added importance. The material idea of a tooth jewelry or an outlined showcase adds a tactile aspect to the demonstration of memory, permitting people to contact, feel, and associate with their past in an unmistakable manner.

The act of making souvenirs from child teeth brings up complex issues and contemplations. Moral worries might emerge as people consider the change of human body parts, even as little as child teeth, into objects of decoration. Others might wrestle with the idea of changelessness, contemplating whether these souvenirs will persevere through time and ages or then again assuming they will, similar to adolescence itself, blur into the openings of memory. These inquiries add layers of consideration to the work on, welcoming people to ponder the idea of connection, the progression of time, and the social subtleties that shape their viewpoints.

The nostalgic worth of child teeth reaches out a long ways past their genuineness, rising above the conventional and flourishing in the significant domains of familial bonds, loved recollections, and the piercing entry of time. Child teeth, those little, fleeting fortunes that mark a kid's change from outset to pre-adulthood, become more than simple organic leftovers — they change into emblematic curios, winding around stories that reverberation the widespread feeling of young life marvel and development. This revered custom of esteeming and protecting child teeth is a social string that traverses ages and various social orders, making an embroidery of shared encounters and aggregate acknowledgment of the valuable idea of these minuscule, ivory-like tokens.

The demonstration of gathering and prizing child teeth is profoundly imbued in social practices all over the planet. Across different practices, the imagery connected to these lost teeth reaches out past the physiological, encapsulating the more extensive idea of development and development. In Western societies, the custom of the tooth pixie imbues the experience of losing child teeth with charm and expectation. Youngsters, with wide-peered toward wonder, fold their fallen teeth underneath their cushions, enthusiastically anticipating the tooth pixie's nighttime visit. The trading of teeth for little gifts or coins changes a basic natural event into an otherworldly transitional experience, and the protected teeth become more than actual pieces — they become keys to the realm of young life charm.

While the tooth pixie is an eccentric person in Western practices, different societies overall have their special traditions related with child teeth. In a few Asian societies, for example, there are customs including the removal of lost teeth. It is normal for kids to toss their lost teeth onto the rooftop or cover them, representing a wish areas of strength for solid grown-up teeth to fill in their place.

These different practices add to a rich embroidery of worldwide customs, each conveying its own imagery and social importance. However, underneath the surface varieties, the consistent idea remains — an affirmation of the transitory idea of young life and the groundbreaking excursion from diaper days to youthfulness.

The remembrances made from child teeth manifest in a variety of structures, filling in as unmistakable articulations of the wistfulness joined to these small fortunes. One pervasive methodology includes hanging the little teeth into pieces of jewelry or arm bands, making wearable charms that exemplify the recollections of young life. The cadenced example of teeth hung together turns into a visual portrayal of development and change, a small scale timetable of a kid's formative process.

Adornments settings offer one more enamoring road for protecting child teeth, changing them into pendants or charms that convey both stylish and nostalgic worth. The craftsmanship engaged with setting these fragile teeth into adornments lifts the tokens into smaller than expected treasures, close impressions of the wearer's very own account. These pieces serve as enhancements as well as unmistakable associations with the blamelessness and marvel of young life.

For the people who lean toward a more enlivening showcase, child teeth frequently find a spot in shadow boxes or edges, joined by photos or other memorabilia. This approach makes a visual scene that protects the teeth as well as fills in as an enamoring piece of craftsmanship. These showcases become central focuses in homes, igniting discussions and welcoming watchers into the nostalgic universe of cherished recollections.

As of late, the deep rooted custom of safeguarding child teeth has embraced advancement through customized and specially crafted adornments. Craftsmans and gem dealers team up with people to create tailor made pieces that exhibit the uniqueness of every tooth as well as integrate extra components, for example, birthstones or initials. This contemporary methodology guarantees that the souvenirs line up with individual stories and inclinations, offering a customized and current wind to an immortal practice.

The wistfulness joined to mementos produced using child teeth stretches out past the actual ancient rarities themselves. These little fortunes become storehouses of recollections, exemplifying the giggling, the tears, and the development that characterize the excursion from earliest stages to puberty. The demonstration of making souvenirs isn't only a conservation of actual remainders; it is a festival of the elusive pith of youth, an acknowledgment of the significant close to home importance joined to these apparently commonplace parts.

Making souvenirs from child teeth is a profoundly private and close cycle, frequently embraced by guardians in a joint effort with their youngsters. The demonstration of gathering a tooth, putting away it with care, and later changing it into a token turns into a common encounter that fortifies the parent-youngster bond. It is a token of adoration and responsibility, a substantial articulation of the craving to clutch the valuable minutes that get away all excessively fast.

As kids effectively partake all the while, the production of souvenirs turns into a type of narrating. Every tooth, with its novel shape and size, conveys its own story — a story of versatility, of developing torments, and of the unyielding walk toward development. Guardians and youngsters wind up returning to these accounts, thinking back about the narratives behind each fallen tooth and the captivating tooth pixie visits that additional a dash of sorcery to the customary.

The nostalgia related with making remembrances from child teeth isn't bound to a solitary social setting. Across the globe, various customs and convictions join on the common experience of life as a youngster and the widespread idea of losing child teeth. In a few Asian societies, for instance, fallen teeth are frequently covered as opposed to left for the tooth pixie, with the conviction that this act will areas of strength for guarantee solid grown-up teeth. No matter what the particular traditions, the hidden topic stays steady — the affirmation that the demonstration of losing teeth is a huge and extraordinary piece of a youngster's excursion.

The formation of remembrances from child teeth additionally crosses with the more extensive talk on memory and the manners by which people decide to celebrate their background. In a world immersed with computerized ephemera, the rawness of remembrances takes on added importance. The material idea of a tooth neckband or an outlined presentation adds a tactile aspect to the demonstration of memory, permitting people to contact, feel, and interface with their past in an unmistakable manner.

The act of making souvenirs from child teeth brings up complex issues and contemplations. Moral worries might emerge as people mull over the change of human body parts, even as little as child teeth, into objects of embellishment.

Others might wrestle with the idea of changelessness, contemplating whether these tokens will persevere through time and ages or on the other hand in the event that they will, similar to adolescence itself, blur into the openings of memory. These inquiries add layers of consideration to the work on, welcoming people to think about the idea of connection, the progression of time, and the social subtleties that shape their viewpoints.

The wistful worth of child teeth is an immortal and culturally diverse affirmation of the transitory idea of experience growing up. From the fanciful notion of tooth pixie visits to the imaginativeness engaged with creating customized gems, the training is a festival of the transient magnificence of youth and the craving to clutch unmistakable tokens of these valuable minutes.

The mementos become more than simple antiques; they advance into storehouses of stories, feelings, and shared encounters, associating people to the charm of experience growing up and the persevering through sorcery of change. As this custom keeps on winding around its way through different societies and ages, it remains as a demonstration of the immortal human tendency to protect the embodiment of youth in unmistakable, persevering through souvenirs.

Chapter 7

Tooth Tales Around the World

Tooth stories from around the world weave a rich embroidery of social convictions, customs, and customs, every one particularly attached to the widespread experience of losing child teeth. Across mainlands and ages, the demonstration of losing teeth is joined by a heap of stories, customs, and fantastical characters that add charm to this common soul changing experience. These tooth stories mirror the variety of human societies as well as highlight the ongoing idea that joins us in perceiving the meaning of this transient stage in adolescence.

In Western societies, one of the most recognizable tooth stories includes the unconventional person known as the tooth pixie. As kids lose their child teeth, they place them underneath their pads around evening time, enthusiastically expecting the appearance of the tooth pixie. In the first part of the day, the lost tooth is supplanted with a little gift or a coin, making an otherworldly trade that delights youngsters and adds a dash of marvel to the most common way of growing up. The tooth pixie, with her ethereal presence, turns into a generous figure related with the section from youth to pre-adulthood.

In Hispanic societies, a comparative tooth-driven custom takes on a remarkable contort. Rather than a tooth pixie, kids frequently place their lost teeth in a glass of water by their bedside. The following morning, they find that the tooth has been supplanted with a little gift or cash. This variety adds a social subtlety to the tooth pixie story, mirroring the assorted manners by which various social orders mix their own sorcery into the experience of losing child teeth.

Asian societies, as well, contribute their own unmistakable tooth stories. In Japan, it is normal for youngsters to toss their lost teeth onto the rooftop or under the floor, joined by a wish serious areas of strength for, substitution teeth. This act is established in the conviction that as the new teeth develop, they will be moved back to the first place where the old ones were disposed of. It's a mix of fables and common sense, representing a longing for hearty grown-up teeth.

In certain pieces of India, a mouse is the supernatural being related with lost teeth. Youngsters place their fallen teeth in a mouse opening or a little holder close to their beds, accepting that the tooth mouse will come and remove the teeth, leaving a gift consequently. This unusual person adds a fun loving aspect to the social stories encompassing child teeth.

African societies, with their rich oral customs, likewise have interesting tooth stories. In certain districts, a typical practice includes covering the lost tooth in the ground, with the conviction that this act will guarantee the tooth's smooth section to existence in the wake of death. This association between child teeth and familial customs features the social significance put on this normal event, mixing it with a feeling of progression and respect for legacy.

The Eskimo public have their own tooth stories, including a powerful person known as the "Moon Man." As indicated by their legends, when a youngster loses a tooth, they hurl it to the moon, asking the Moon Man to send them another one. This innovative story mirrors the cozy association between social convictions, divine bodies, and the groundbreaking system of growing up.

In the Center East, especially in nations like Iran, the practice of praising the deficiency of child teeth is known as "Nahaan." During this festival, loved ones assemble to stamp the event, and the youngster's lost tooth is put in a beautiful compartment. The occasion is frequently joined by customs and petitions, under-scoring the social and familial meaning of this regular formative achievement.

The variety of tooth stories all over the planet reaches out past the social and provincial varieties. It likewise dives into the domain of legendary animals and fantastical creatures that assume a part in the stories encompassing lost child teeth. For example, in the Celtic custom, pixies are accepted to have a distinct fascination with human teeth. Youngsters would leave their lost teeth outside, and it was accepted that the pixies would gather them for different purposes, like structure their otherworldly abodes.

In South African old stories, the tooth pixie appears as a little bird known as the "Tooth Mouse." Like other tooth stories, kids place their lost teeth in an assigned spot, and the Tooth Mouse is said to gather the teeth, abandoning a little gift. This inventive bend on the tooth pixie topic grandstands the social variety inside a landmass.

These worldwide tooth stories not just feature the creative manners by which social orders have woven accounts around the deficiency of child teeth yet in addition uncover the social qualities and convictions related with this regular peculiarity. From pixies and mice to the moon and familial spirits, every tooth story mirrors the remarkable viewpoints and imaginative articulations of various societies in embracing and commending the progress from diaper days to adolescence.

Past the domain of fables and social stories, the act of saving and honoring child teeth takes on different structures around the world. In many societies, guardians and youngsters take part in the formation of souvenirs as an unmistakable articulation of the wistful worth connected to these little, ivory-like fortunes. The teeth are frequently hung into pieces of jewelry or wristbands, changing them into wearable images of development and recollections.

Adornments settings, like pendants or charms, give one more road to saving and showing child teeth. The craftsmanship associated with setting these sensitive teeth into adornments lifts them into smaller than normal show-stoppers, embodying the excellence and uniqueness of every tooth. These pieces act as enhancements as well as become esteemed legacies, went down through ages, conveying with them the accounts and opinions of family ancestry.

Shadow boxes and approaches offer a more embellishing way to deal with showing child teeth, frequently joined by photos and other memorabilia. These showcases become visual narratives of young life, catching the quintessence of development and change. The plan of teeth in imaginative introductions changes the normal demonstration of losing child teeth into a type of creative articulation, recognizing a huge section in a kid's life.

Lately, the coming of customized and hand crafted gems has carried a contemporary turn to the well established custom of safeguarding child teeth. Craftsmans and gem dealers team up with people to make tailor made pieces that exhibit the uniqueness of every tooth as well as consolidate extra components, for example, birthstones or initials. This cutting edge approach guarantees that the mementos line up with individual stories and inclinations, adding a layer of personalization to the immortal practice.

The nostalgic worth of child teeth, as communicated through these worldwide tooth stories and various acts of conservation, addresses the significant close to home association that people and social orders trait to the excursion from earliest stages to youth.

The demonstration of losing child teeth turns into a common encounter that rises above social limits, joining humankind in the acknowledgment of the temporary idea of young life and the immortal meaning of development and change.

As people across the globe keep on winding around their own tooth stories and make souvenirs to honor this general soul changing experience, the practice stays a demonstration of the persevering through human longing to celebrate and protect the sorcery of young life. Whether through the impulsive notion of tooth pixies, the imagery of heavenly creatures, or the creative stories of social fables, tooth stories all over the planet highlight the common perspective that horrible child teeth isn't simply a natural event yet a significant and valued second in the embroidery of human experience.

7.1. Cultural Perspectives

Social viewpoints offer a multi-layered focal point through which people and social orders decipher, comprehend, and explore their general surroundings. The rich embroidery of human societies, formed by history, customs, and shared encounters, adds to a different mosaic of viewpoints that impact convictions, values, and connections. Investigating social points of view is a multifaceted excursion that uncovers the intricacies and subtleties of the human experience, uncovering how people and networks make importance of their reality, draw in with others, and shape their aggregate personalities.

One of the major parts of social viewpoints is the impact of social qualities on individual and aggregate ways of behaving. Values, profoundly instilled through childhood and cultural standards, act as core values that shape how people focus on, see ethical quality, and characterize what is significant. For example, individualistic societies, common in Western social orders, frequently focus on independence, individual accomplishment, and individual freedoms. Conversely, collectivist societies, normal in numerous Asian social orders, underline public congruity, relationship, and gathering attachment.

These different social qualities add to unmistakable methodologies in regions, for example, training, direction, and relational connections. In individualistic societies, achievement might be estimated by private achievements, and navigation frequently focuses on private inclinations and independence. In collectivist societies, achievement might be entwined with family or local area accomplishments, and choices might be made in light of the more extensive gathering's prosperity. Understanding these subtleties is critical for encouraging multifaceted correspondence and joint effort, as it empowers people to explore and value different social scenes.

Language, as a key component of culture, assumes a crucial part in molding points of view. The words and articulations extraordinary to a language frequently epitomize social subtleties, reflecting verifiable occasions, social designs, and aggregate convictions. Semantic relativity, an idea proposing that language impacts thought, highlights how the dialects we talk shape the manner in which we see and order the world. For instance, a few dialects might have words that exemplify socially unambiguous ideas, offering experiences into the qualities and needs of a specific culture.

Besides, social viewpoints are significantly interwoven with the idea of time. The manner in which various societies see and worth time differs fundamentally. In certain societies, time is viewed as direct and scant, provoking an emphasis on effectiveness, reliability, and future-situated arranging. Different societies might embrace a more recurrent perspective on time, putting significance on the current second, musicality, and interconnectedness with nature. These fleeting directions impact day to day propensities, hard working attitudes, and cultural assumptions, molding how people focus on and distribute their time.

Strict and otherworldly convictions likewise assume a urgent part in molding social viewpoints. The world's religions offer different structures for grasping presence, ethical quality, and the motivation behind life. These conviction frameworks impact people's moral contemplations, how they might interpret enduring and bliss, and their view of the consecrated. For instance, Eastern methods of reasoning like Buddhism might accentuate the temporariness of life and the quest for inward harmony, while Abrahamic religions like Christianity, Judaism, and Islam frequently center around divine direction, moral codes, and eternity.

Social points of view stretch out to the domain of feel, impacting imaginative articulations, style, and the enthusiasm for excellence. What is viewed as stylishly satisfying differs generally across societies, reflecting different sensibilities and verifiable impacts. Understanding these distinctions is fundamental for cultivating diverse appreciation and staying away from ethnocentrism, where one's social focal point is utilized as the norm to pass judgment on others.

With regards to relational peculiarities, social viewpoints significantly impact familial designs, jobs, and assumptions. The meaning of family itself can change, for certain societies accentuating more distant family organizations and shared bonds, while others focus on family unit units. Social assumptions about orientation jobs, obedient devotion, and intergenerational connections shape the elements inside families and impact people's characters and life decisions.

Social points of view on instruction give knowledge into the qualities a general public holds dear. Various societies might focus on different parts of instruction, like repetition remembrance, decisive reasoning, or all encompassing turn of events. The objectives of schooling, the job of instructors, and the accentuation on scholarly accomplishment versus character improvement all reflect social qualities and assumptions. Perceiving these varieties is critical for instructors and policymakers to make comprehensive and viable schooling systems.

Social points of view are likewise clear in ways to deal with wellbeing and health. Customary recuperating rehearses, dietary propensities, and perspectives toward psychological well-being can differ essentially starting with one culture then onto the next. A few societies might put areas of strength for an on preventive measures and comprehensive prosperity, while others might depend on clinical mediations and specific medicines. Understanding these points of view is fundamental for medical services experts to give socially capable and delicate consideration.

The impact of social viewpoints is especially clear in the manner social orders explore relational connections. Correspondence styles, articulations of feelings, and standards in regards to individual space can contrast altogether between societies. High-setting societies, where correspondence depends on implied signs and shared setting, may appear differently in relation to low-setting societies, where express verbal correspondence is underlined. These distinctions can prompt misconceptions and misinterpretations, highlighting the significance of diverse relational abilities.

Social viewpoints likewise shape mentalities toward power, administration, and administration. A few societies might esteem progressive designs, regard to power figures, and an aggregate liability regarding keeping up with social concordance. Others might focus on populism, participatory direction, and individual freedoms. These viewpoints impact political frameworks, administration models, and the assumptions residents have of their chiefs.

In the domain of innovation and advancement, social points of view add to different ways to deal with critical thinking and imagination. A few societies might esteem individual creativity and chance taking, cultivating a culture of business and development. Others might focus on cooperative endeavors, agreement building, and steady advancement. Perceiving and valuing these different methodologies is fundamental for encouraging a worldwide climate helpful for development and progress.

Social points of view on nature and the climate are additionally different. A few societies might see nature as an asset to be tackled and dominated, while others might consider it to be a hallowed substance to be worshipped and safeguarded. These viewpoints impact ecological strategies, protection endeavors, and perspectives toward supportable living. Connecting these viewpoints is pivotal for tending to worldwide difficulties, for example, environmental change and biodiversity misfortune.

The effect of globalization on social viewpoints is a dynamic and developing peculiarity. As the world turns out to be progressively interconnected, societies collaborate, mix, and impact each other. While globalization can prompt social homogenization in certain angles, it additionally presents potential open doors for diverse trade, shared advancement, and the development of new social half breeds. Exploring the harmony between saving social variety and embracing worldwide interconnectedness is a perplexing test looked by social orders around the world.

Social points of view additionally impact reactions to misfortune and emergency. Various societies might have differing survival techniques, strength systems, and translations of misery. Social standards in regards to looking for help, communicating feelings, and local area support assume a vital part in molding people's and networks' reactions to challenges. Understanding these elements is fundamental for offering compelling help and mediation in the midst of emergency.

Social points of view, well established in history and formed by assorted customs, keep on impacting each feature of human existence. The complex interaction of social qualities, convictions, and standards adds to the manner in which people see reality, draw in with others, and build their characters. Diving further into the domain of social points of view, one experiences the powerful idea of these impacts across different areas.

In the domain of financial matters, social points of view manifest in perspectives toward work, business, and abundance. A few societies might put a high worth on enterprising nature, monetary achievement, and material collection as signs of individual accomplishment. Conversely, others might focus on a fair and manageable methodology, seeing abundance with regards to local area prosperity and social obligation. These social viewpoints shape monetary frameworks, strategic policies, and individual yearnings.

Social viewpoints likewise make a permanent imprint on imaginative articulations, affecting the creation and understanding of writing, music, visual expressions, and performing expressions. Various societies celebrate assorted types of imaginative magnificence, narrating, and imagery, mirroring their special verifiable accounts and cultural qualities. The enthusiasm for craftsmanship turns into a focal point through which one can look into the aggregate soul of a culture, catching the substance of its inventiveness and creative mind.

Besides, social points of view assume a significant part in forming cultural mentalities toward inclusivity, variety, and civil rights. A few societies might focus on populist standards, effectively looking to embrace and celebrate variety in the entirety of its structures. Others might wrestle with verifiable inheritances that have propagated disparities, requiring purposeful endeavors to encourage inclusivity. Exploring these intricate elements requests a nuanced comprehension of social viewpoints to construct social orders that are evenhanded and just.

Social points of view reach out to the space of morals and profound quality, affecting the comprehension of good and bad, ethicalness and bad habit. Various societies might have fluctuating moral structures that guide people in exploring moral difficulties. The social setting shapes the ethical compass, affecting choices with respect to trustworthiness, honesty, and the treatment of others. Perceiving the variety of moral viewpoints cultivates multifaceted comprehension and moral discourse.

With regards to customs and functions, social points of view shape the manners by which people mark critical life altering situations, changes, and achievements. Birth, marriage, demise, and different transitional experiences are permeated with social importance, imagery, and formal practices that fluctuate generally across social orders. These customs act as social standards, supporting a feeling of character, having a place, and coherence.

Social points of view likewise impact the manner in which social orders approach and see wellbeing and prosperity. Customary mending rehearses, perspectives toward emotional well-being, and dietary propensities are many times well established in social convictions. Understanding these viewpoints is fundamental for planning medical care frameworks that are socially delicate and receptive to the assorted requirements and upsides of various networks.

Moreover, the job of elderly folks and the idea of insight change fundamentally across societies, impacting familial designs and intergenerational connections. In certain societies, older folks are venerated for their background and are viewed as wellsprings of shrewdness and direction. In others, energy might be all the more exceptionally esteemed, with an accentuation on advancement and versatility. These social viewpoints shape cultural mentalities toward maturing, providing care, and the exchange of information between ages.

Social points of view likewise assume a critical part in the ways people and social orders draw in with innovation and logical headways. A few societies might move toward mechanical development with energy, seeing it for of progress and improvement. Others might move toward it with alert, taking into account the expected moral and social ramifications. Understanding these viewpoints is fundamental for making innovation that lines up with different social qualities and needs.

In the worldwide setting, the transaction of social viewpoints turns out to be considerably more mind boggling as societies experience each other through relocation, exchange, and correspondence. The peculiarity of social trade and multifaceted associations presents new layers of impact, testing prior social standards and encouraging the rise of half breed social characters. Exploring these experiences requires an elevated familiarity with social responsiveness, regard, and an eagerness to participate in significant discourse.

As social orders keep on wrestling with the difficulties and amazing open doors introduced by social points of view, the significance of encouraging intercultural skill turns out to be progressively clear. Intercultural skill includes the capacity to comprehend, appreciate, and actually explore social contrasts. It requires a readiness to participate in self-reflection, challenge social predispositions, and embrace the wealth that variety brings to the human experience.

Taking everything into account, social viewpoints are an unpredictable snare of impacts that shape the manners in which people and social orders decipher, explore, and add to the world. From financial frameworks to creative articulations, from morals to medical care, and from intergenerational connections to innovative progressions, social points of view imbue each part of human existence with importance and importance. Embracing social variety requires a pledge to figuring out, regard, and liberality, encouraging a worldwide local area that esteems the extravagance of human encounters across societies. As the world keeps on developing, the investigation of social points of view stays a dynamic and continuous excursion toward building a more interconnected, sympathetic, and amicable worldwide society.

7.2. Variations in tooth-related traditions globally

Varieties in tooth-related customs universally offer a captivating knowledge into the different ways societies across the world see and commend the regular peculiarity of losing child teeth. This widespread soul changing experience, set apart by the progress from essential to super durable teeth, has led to a variety of customs, customs, and fables that mirror the remarkable social characters and verifiable settings of various social orders.

In Western societies, the tooth pixie becomes the overwhelming focus as a darling and unconventional person related with the deficiency of child teeth. Kids, with wide-peered toward expectation, place their fallen teeth underneath their cushions, anticipating the nighttime visit of the tooth pixie. In the first part of the day, the lost tooth is mysteriously supplanted with a little gift or coin. This charming custom changes a routine organic event into a mysterious encounter, making enduring recollections for kids and supporting the feeling of marvel related with youth.

Hispanic societies offer an unmistakable variety to the tooth pixie custom. Rather than setting the lost tooth under the cushion, kids frequently drench their teeth in a glass of water by their bedside. The following morning, they find that the tooth has been supplanted with a little gift or cash. This variety adds a social subtlety to the tooth pixie story, exhibiting the variety in the ways various social orders imbue sorcery into the most common way of losing child teeth.

In Asian societies, tooth-related customs are different and established in social imagery. In Japan, for example, youngsters participate in the custom of tossing their lost teeth onto the rooftop or under the floor. Joined by a wish areas of strength for solid substitution teeth, this training represents a consistent progress from child teeth to grown-up teeth. The demonstration of tossing the teeth onto the rooftop or covering them mirrors a social faith in guaranteeing the imperativeness and strength of the arising grown-up teeth.

A few Asian societies, remembering those for China and Korea, have customs related with the removal of lost teeth. It is normal for youngsters to cover their lost teeth in unambiguous areas, like the nursery or a pruned plant. The conviction basic this training is that covering the teeth guarantees the development of solid and sound grown-up teeth in their place. These practices highlight the social importance connected to the progress from essential to long-lasting teeth.

In India, tooth-related customs are frequently entwined with social and strict practices. A few families decide to cover the lost teeth in the ground, while others might drench them in streams or different waterways. The decision of custom is much of the time impacted by social convictions and territorial traditions, mirroring the different embroidered artwork of customs inside the country.

African societies contribute their own remarkable tooth-related customs, frequently with associations with tribal convictions. In specific locales, it is standard to cover the lost tooth in the ground with the conviction that this act guarantees a smooth section for the tooth to existence in the wake of death. The association between child teeth and familial customs features the social significance put on this regular event, implanting it with a feeling of coherence and love for legacy.

In Eskimo fables, a person known as the "Moon Man" assumes a focal part in tooth-related customs. As indicated by this custom, when a kid loses a tooth, they hurl it to the moon, asking the Moon Man to send them another one. This inventive story mirrors the close association between social convictions, heavenly bodies, and the extraordinary course of growing up.

Center Eastern societies, especially in nations like Iran, praise the deficiency of child teeth with a custom known as "Nahaan." During this festival, loved ones accumulate to check the event, and the youngster's lost tooth is set in an improving compartment. The occasion frequently includes ceremonies and petitions, accentuating the social and familial meaning of this regular formative achievement.

The variety of tooth-related customs additionally reaches out to South American societies. In a few native networks, youngsters take part in ceremonies including the entombment or presenting of lost teeth. These practices frequently have social and otherworldly importance, interfacing the demonstration of losing child teeth to more extensive subjects of development, change, and the recurrent idea of life.

In the Maori culture of New Zealand, an exceptional custom includes the entombment of lost teeth. Maori youngsters are urged to cover their lost teeth in the ground, and explicit customs might go with this training. The association between the earth and the teeth is emblematic, mirroring the Maori perspective and their profound regard for the indigenous habitat.

In contemporary times, the globalized world has seen the development of present day varieties in tooth-related customs. The tooth pixie, while established in Western old stories, has turned into a well known and embraced figure in many societies all over the planet. The idea of a kind being trading lost teeth for little gifts or cash has risen above social limits, making a common encounter for kids in different social orders.

Past these social varieties, the act of saving child teeth has acquired notoriety as of late. Many guardians, perceiving the wistful worth connected to these little fortunes, participate in making remembrances like accessories, wristbands, or outlined shows. These mementos act as unmistakable tokens of the short lived nature of life as a youngster and the extraordinary excursion from childhood to immaturity.

The nostalgia appended to tooth-related customs goes past the actual demonstration of losing child teeth; it includes the more extensive subjects of development, change, and the progression of time. Whether through capricious characters like the tooth pixie or socially established ceremonies like covering teeth in the ground, these practices act as social touchpoints that associate ages and networks.

The varieties in tooth-related customs worldwide feature the lavishness of social variety and the horde manners by which social orders imbue significance into apparently ordinary parts of life. From the lively wizardry of the tooth pixie to the well established ceremonies associated with tribal convictions, these customs offer looks into the social woven artwork that winds around together the common human experience of growing up. As societies proceed to develop and cross, tooth-related customs stand as getting through markers of social character, spanning the past and the present in a festival of the widespread excursion from youth to adulthood.

The varieties in tooth-related customs worldwide are a demonstration of the rich embroidery of social variety that characterizes human social orders. In investigating these practices further, it becomes clear that the ceremonies and convictions encompassing the deficiency of child teeth reach out past simple old stories — they embody further social qualities, verifiable accounts, and the immortal human undertaking to track down significance in normal peculiarities.

Across many societies in Asia, the demonstration of losing child teeth is much of the time joined by exceptional ceremonies that mirror a mix of social imagery and down to earth convictions. In Japan, the practice of tossing lost teeth onto the rooftop or under the floor is pull in the wish major areas of strength for sound substitution teeth. This training fills in as a substantial articulation of the social faith in the interconnectedness between the actual demonstration of losing teeth and the ideal result of strong grown-up teeth.

In India, the tooth mouse becomes the dominant focal point in tooth-related customs. Kids place their lost teeth in an assigned spot, and the tooth mouse is accepted to come and remove the teeth, abandoning a little gift. This capricious person adds a perky aspect to the social stories encompassing child teeth, underlining the creative manners by which societies imbue wizardry into the ordinary encounters of life as a youngster.

In numerous African societies, the demonstration of covering lost teeth in the ground is a typical practice. The conviction that this custom guarantees a smooth section for the tooth to existence in the wake of death mirrors the social importance put on the change from child teeth to grown-up teeth. The association between this normal event and tribal customs highlights the all encompassing manner by which societies coordinate the patterns of life into their conviction frameworks.

The Eskimo public, with their special social setting, have an unmistakable tooth-related custom including the "Moon Man." The demonstration of hurling a lost tooth to the moon and asking the Moon Man to send another one isn't simply an eccentric story yet an impression of how social convictions and heavenly bodies entwine in the narrating of various social orders.

In the Center East, the practice of "Nahaan" in nations like Iran includes a festival of the deficiency of child teeth. The lost tooth is set in an embellishing compartment, and the occasion is set apart by customs and petitions. This social practice underlines the mutual and familial meaning of formative achievements, interlacing the individual with the system.

Varieties in tooth-related customs additionally stretch out to South American societies, where native networks might take part in ceremonies including the entombment or presenting of lost teeth. These practices frequently convey profound and social importance, adjusting the demonstration of losing child teeth with more extensive subjects of association with nature, development, and the patterns of life.

While these conventional practices keep on flourishing in many societies, the globalization of mainstream society has presented a cutting edge and broadly embraced tooth-related custom — the tooth pixie. Established in Western legends, the tooth pixie has turned into a general figure, charming kids all over the planet with the commitment of little gifts or cash in return for their lost teeth. This cutting edge variety rises above social limits, making a common encounter for kids in different social orders and adding to the globalized story of experience growing up enchantment.

Notwithstanding these social and territorial varieties, the act of protecting child teeth has picked up speed in contemporary times. Many guardians perceive the wistful worth joined to these little, ivory-like fortunes and participate in making customized remembrances. Whether it be hanging teeth into adornments, outlining them in shadow boxes, or integrating them into tailor made bits of craftsmanship, these remembrances act as substantial articulations of the profound association people and families have to the passing snapshots of young life.

The wistfulness appended to tooth-related customs, whether established in antiquated old stories or adjusted to present day sensibilities, highlights the general subjects of development, change, and the progression of time. These practices act as social touchpoints that interface ages, winding around a story that rises above individual encounters and addresses the common human excursion from earliest stages to pre-adulthood.

All in all, varieties in tooth-related customs universally uncover the assorted and creative manners by which societies across the world praise the regular progress from child teeth to super durable teeth. Whether through eccentric characters like the tooth pixie, socially attached ceremonies that interface with genealogical convictions, or contemporary acts of making customized remembrances, these practices epitomize the quintessence of social variety and the all inclusive longing to imbue importance into the achievements of human turn of events. As social orders proceed to develop and meet, tooth-related customs stand as getting through markers of social personality, mirroring the aggregate insight, imagination, and flexibility of different societies all over the planet.

7.3. Uniqueness and commonalities in diverse cultures

Uniqueness and shared characteristics in different societies comprise the mind boggling embroidery of human development, winding around together a mosaic of customs, convictions, and customs that mirror the common and unmistakable features of the human experience.

Investigating the rich variety of societies internationally divulges a complicated exchange of verifiable heritages, topographical impacts, and socio-social elements that shape the remarkable personality of every local area while at the same time uncovering the widespread strings that interface mankind.

The uniqueness of each culture is well established in its set of experiences, giving a logical focal point through which customs and customs are passed down from one age to another. Authentic occasions, relocations, and communications with adjoining social orders engrave particular engravings on social practices. For instance, the social wealth of China is complicatedly attached to its old progress, set apart by significant philosophical practices, many-sided works of art, for example, calligraphy and silk painting, and a language that conveys the heaviness of millennia of recorded history. The uniqueness of Chinese culture lies in its old roots as well as in its capacity to develop and adjust while holding serious areas of strength for an of personality.

Also, the native societies of the Americas grandstand the strength and variety that rise up out of hundreds of years of transformation to various biological systems. From the Inuit people group in the Icy to the Amazonian clans in South America, each native gathering has a one of a kind arrangement of customs, dialects, and otherworldly practices that are personally associated with their particular surroundings. The Inuit, for example, have created multifaceted information on getting by in unforgiving Icy circumstances, while the Amazonian clans have a significant comprehension of the different vegetation of the rainforest, molding their social practices and convictions.

Strict and profound convictions contribute fundamentally to the uniqueness of societies. The variety of strict practices all over the planet, from the polytheistic customs of Hinduism to the monotheistic religions of Judaism, Christianity, and Islam, mirrors the horde manners by which social orders look to grasp the heavenly and the reason for human life. The rich woven artwork of strict practices includes customs, celebrations, and moral rules that shape the ethical texture of networks. For instance, the dynamic celebrations of Diwali in India, Hanukkah in Jewish people group, Christmas in Christian customs, and Eid in Islam exhibit the one of a kind manners by which various societies praise their otherworldly convictions.

Social articulations through craftsmanship, writing, and music act as strong vehicles for conveying the novel personality of a local area. The unpredictable dance types of old style Indian dance, the suggestive artworks of the Renaissance in Europe, the conventional narrating of native societies, and the musical thumps of African drumming are articulations of the particular manners by which societies convey their accounts, values, and feel. These imaginative articulations mirror the inventiveness of a local area as well as act as storehouses of social legacy, communicating information and personality across ages.

Language, as a transporter of culture, is a principal part of uniqueness. The world's dialects, numbering in the large numbers, offer different approaches to offering viewpoints, feelings, and social subtleties. The apparent intricacies of Mandarin Chinese, the melodious excellence of Arabic calligraphy, and the polysynthetic construction of Inuit dialects are instances of etymological variety that shape the extraordinary character of societies. Language works with correspondence as well as conveys the elusive components of social personality, protecting the insight, humor, and ethos of a local area.

Culinary practices give one more window into the uniqueness of societies. The fixings, cooking techniques, and flavors that characterize a food are in many cases well established in the topographical and verifiable setting of a locale. The zesty and fragrant dishes of Indian cooking, the fragile kinds of Japanese sushi, the generous and various contributions of Italian pasta, and the rich and differed flavors of Center Eastern dishes all add to the culinary uniqueness that mirrors the social personality of every local area. Culinary practices likewise act as a type of social tact, encouraging diverse figuring out through the all inclusive delight of sharing a feast.

While the uniqueness of societies is a wellspring of pride and character, it coincides with the shared traits that tight spot humankind together. These common components cut across geological, semantic, and verifiable limits, framing the reason for grasping, compassion, and worldwide participation.

The human experience is set apart by normal topics that resound across societies. Love, satisfaction, distress, and the quest for joy are general goals that rise above social contrasts. The festival of life achievements like birth, marriage, and demise, frequently joined by customs and services, is a shared trait that highlights the common human experience. Whether it be the blissful festivals of a wedding function in India, the serious customs of a Japanese tea service, or the energetic celebrations of Fair in Brazil, the quintessence of these minutes mirrors the general craving for association, importance, and having a place.

Besides, the human limit with respect to inventiveness, development, and narrating fills in as an ongoing idea that ties societies together. The narrating customs of old civic establishments, whether through oral legends, composed writing, or visual expressions, have added to the aggregate repository of human insight and creative mind. The getting through allure of fantasies, tales, and legends across societies addresses the common human interest with accounts that investigate the intricacies of presence, profound quality, and the secrets of the universe.

The essential qualities that support human social orders — like equity, reasonableness, sympathy, and regard for other people — structure a typical moral establishment. While the declarations of these qualities might fluctuate across societies, the hidden standards join mankind as its continued looking for a fair and agreeable presence. Moral frameworks, whether explained through strict lessons, philosophical customs, or social standards, shape human connections and guide people in their ethical decisions.

The quest for information and the mission for understanding the regular world are all inclusive undertakings that rise above social limits. Logical request, numerical disclosures, and mechanical progressions are cooperative endeavors that draw upon the common interest and keenness of humankind. The commitments of researchers, mathematicians, and pioneers from assorted societies have altogether enhanced the worldwide pool of information, cultivating progress and development to support all.

Human feelings, communicated through craftsmanship, writing, and music, structure a general language that reverberates across societies. The reminiscent force of a melodic structure, the nuanced brushstrokes of a canvas, or the impactful expressions of a sonnet have the ability to summon shared feelings and interface people across social partitions. The comprehensiveness of close to home articulation highlights the normal humankind that ties individuals together, rising above the obstructions of language and social particularity.

Besides, the interconnectedness of the cutting edge world, worked with by progressions in correspondence, transportation, and innovation, has led to a worldwide cognizance. The familiarity with shared difficulties, for example, environmental change, general wellbeing emergencies, and civil rights issues has prompted an expanded feeling of worldwide relationship. The shared characteristic of these difficulties calls for cooperative arrangements that draw upon the aggregate insight and assets of different societies.

The exchange among uniqueness and shared characteristics in different societies is a dynamic and developing embroidery that characterizes the intricacy of human life. In digging further into the subtleties of social variety, it becomes obvious that the concurrence of uniqueness and shared components shapes the establishment for culturally diverse figuring out, sympathy, and the potential for an agreeable worldwide local area.

Uniqueness, established in the verifiable, topographical, and social settings of each culture, offers a kaleidoscope of customs, ceremonies, and articulations that recognize one local area from another. The kaleidoscope turns as one analyzes the complexities of the Holi celebration in India, with its dynamic tones representing the victory of good over evil, or the musical and profound moves of the Sufi custom in the Center East. These interesting social articulations not just mirror the imagination and character of a specific local area yet additionally act as windows into the more extensive human limit with respect to variety and variation.

Social uniqueness is likewise appeared in the perplexing connections among networks and their common habitats. The native societies of the Icy, like the Inuit, have created perplexing information and practices that empower them to explore the brutal states of their current circumstance.

The interesting beneficial interaction between the Maasai nation of East Africa and their dairy cattle mirrors an amicable conjunction with nature, molding their social practices and conventional lifestyle. These models show how social uniqueness is frequently profoundly entwined with the natural settings wherein social orders develop.

Strict variety further adds to the uniqueness of societies, offering a horde of profound points of view that shape perspectives, values, and moral systems. The complex ceremonies of Hindu celebrations, the thoughtful acts of Buddhist practices, and the public petitions of Islamic social orders feature the assorted manners by which societies express their otherworldly convictions. These strict practices not just give a feeling of personality and motivation yet additionally add to the social texture by cultivating an aggregate feeling of significance and greatness.

Then again, shared traits among different societies structure the propensities that associate humankind in its common process through reality. The general subjects of affection, family, and the quest for satisfaction are ageless desires that reverberation across societies, rising above semantic and social obstructions. The festival of life achievements, like birth, marriage, and demise, through customs and functions, features the normal human experience of stamping huge minutes with shared social articulations.

Besides, the worldwide interconnectedness worked with by present day correspondence and travel has made a common social cognizance. The trading of thoughts, customs, and impacts across borders has prompted the rise of a worldwide culture that consolidates components from different practices. Well known music, movies, design, and food frequently mirror this blend, delineating how social shared traits can encourage a feeling of shared worldwide character.

The quest for information and development fills in as one more binding together power among different societies. Logical disclosures, mechanical progressions, and scholarly accomplishments are cooperative undertakings that draw upon the aggregate keenness of mankind. The comprehensiveness of the logical strategy and the common journey for understanding the normal world add to a worldwide pool of information that rises above social and geological limits.

Moral standards and virtues, while communicated through different social focal points, frequently merge on principal ideas of equity, reasonableness, and empathy. The Brilliant Rule, tracked down in varieties in numerous social and strict customs, embodies the common moral rules that guide human associations and connections. While social settings might shape the utilization of these qualities, the basic obligation to moral lead stays a consistent idea across different social orders.